What's the Big Deal About OTHER RELIGIONS?

John Ankerberg
& Dillon Burroughs

HARVEST HOUSE PUBLISHERS

EUGENE, OREGON

WHAT'S THE BIG DEAL ABOUT OTHER RELIGIONS?
Copyright © 2008 by John Ankerberg and Dillon Burroughs
Published by Harvest House Publishers
Eugene, Oregon 97402
www.harvesthousepublishers.com

Library of Congress Cataloging-in-Publication Data
Ankerberg, John, 1945-
    What's the big deal about other religions? / John Ankerberg and Dillon Burroughs.
    p. cm.
    Includes bibliographical references.
    ISBN 978-0-7369-2122-0 (pbk.)
    ISBN 978-0-7369-3470-1 (eBook)
    1. Religions. I. Burroughs, Dillon. II. Title.
    BL80.3.A555 2007
    200—dc2

                                                          2007028418

Printed in the United States of America

Contents

Part Four: Eastern Religions

Part Five: Multigod and Anti-God Religions

How to
Use This
Book

What's the Big Deal About Other Religions? is designed not only for *communication,* but also for building *community.* Developed around the major religions and religious movements that influence our world today, these chapters can also stand as the basis of a small discussion group, classroom study, or retreat resource for those desiring to share their learning with others.

At the end of this book, you'll find a discussion guide. Feel free to use these questions as starting points for even further discussion as you seek to understand the diversity among other religions today.

Throughout the pages of this resource, you'll also notice that many of the statistics and detailed quotes are placed in various sidebars. We've intentionally done this to help the text of the book feel more like a conversation. However, we still feel passionate about providing additional research for those desiring more information. We hope that these quotes, statistics, and insights will help supercharge your growth even further.

Third, you'll also find a wide variety of further materials in the "Additional Resources" section—materials that will enhance your understanding of other religions. We've mentioned other books we've written on world religions, several top Web sites that are good for personal study, and links to the best online articles from the Ankerberg Theological Research Institute. In addition, we've listed many related video series and transcripts from past episodes of *The John Anker-berg Show* for those who prefer to use audio-visual resources.

Also, we are glad to personally be involved in the learning process with you. Feel free to contact us via e-mail at bigdealaboutother religions@johnankerberg.org with any comments or questions you may have.

Finally, know we are praying with you as you progress in your understanding of the "big deal" about other religions today. We hope your desire to learn matches that of the Bereans in Paul's day. They searched the Scriptures every day to discover whether what they were learning was true (Acts 17:11). God bless you as you begin the adventure of the big deal about other religions.

Why Should
I Care About
Other Religions?

"Don't all religions lead to God?"

"Why should I believe my way is the only way?"

"It doesn't matter what you believe as long as you are sincere, right?"

"Isn't it arrogant to tell someone his or her spiritual beliefs are wrong?"

"Christians are so judgmental. How can they say they have the truth?"

The questions above are asked every day by non-Christians, atheists, agnostics, and even some devout spiritual leaders. Others choose to avoid asking spiritual questions at all. For instance, in a 2006 interview on CNN's *Larry King Live,* actor George Clooney was asked about the issue of faith in his life:

> In talking about religion, if you're well known, anything you say, it sort of ticks off a bunch of other people and attacks their belief. So I always try to say that, you know, first and foremost, that whatever anybody believes as long as it doesn't hurt anybody else, it's fair enough, and works, and I think, is real, and matters. I don't happen to have those beliefs, as much, you know, I don't believe in those things.[1]

Clooney's perspective mirrors the attitudes of millions of others who react to questions about spirituality with the answer, "Whatever you believe is okay as long as it doesn't hurt anyone else." As Harvey Cox, professor at Harvard Divinity School, wrote in *Foreign Policy,* "More and more people view the world's religious traditions as a buffet from which they can pick and choose."[2]

He Said It

"There is only one religion, though there are a hundred versions of it."

—GEORGE BERNARD SHAW[3]

But how authentic is such thinking? Does it really not even matter what a person believes? If you're Muslim, the Qur'an's tradition teaches death to those who refuse to convert (Sura 2:193; 9:29). Jewish custom practices separation from non-Jews. Christianity teaches that only those who choose to receive God's gift of salvation made available through Jesus will spend eternity in heaven. Buddhism teaches reincarnation, while Mormonism talks about fulfilling a specific set of religious practices to reach higher levels of heaven. Atheism believes there is no God; Hinduism believes in thousands of gods. Only one of these groups can be right—for more than one to be correct is not possible because these various teachings contain contradictory ideas.

Is it arrogant for Christians to believe that Christianity is the only true religion? Or for Muslims to teach that the Qur'an is the highest form of truth and all other religions are inferior? Or for Buddhism to have began when Gautama Buddha rejected two of the fundamental teachings of Hinduism? Or for Hinduism to be uncompromising on the law of karma, the authority of the Vedas (their holy texts), and reincarnation? Or for Judaism to reject all other religions and teach that the promised Messiah is still yet to arrive? If any one of these views is true, then the others are false. They cannot all be true at the same time.

Evaluating the Evidence

True seekers ask, as the Roman leader Pilate, "What is truth?"[4] If a religion contradicts the beliefs and practices of another religion in significant ways, then someone is right and someone else is wrong. Sure, many religions share similar moral themes, such as giving to the poor or the concept of meditation or prayer. However, when we look at the diversity of spiritual understandings, it's impossible to find common ground on the issues of how we can enjoy a secure life now or in the afterlife.

Our plan in this book isn't to bash those who sincerely practice acts of good and kindness to others. Rather, our hope is to converse with you about the vast differences between the major world religions. As we discover the monumental variations that exist, we can begin to evaluate our own spiritual beliefs. *What do I believe* about God? The afterlife? Prayer? Sacred books? Spiritual experiences? How can I know what is true?

What Can We Learn from Other Religions?

1. If we are more sensitive to what others believe, we'll interact more effectively with them.

2. Learning about other belief systems helps us appreciate our own faith more.

3. Learning from other religions gives us greater compassion for other people.[5]

We encourage you to brew a mug of your favorite coffee, grab a snack, and kick back to read about the highlights of the major religious movements in our world today. As we engage in this journey, we hope you'll consider how the stories you read connect with your own life story. By the end of our experience, perhaps your story will change to include an enhanced viewpoint of what you believe and practice on these sacred issues.

Before we share together in this spiritual quest, however, we want to be up front in sharing our own stories. We think you'll be surprised at the changes we've encountered personally in our research on other religions.

"Careful examination of the basic tenets of the various religious traditions demonstrates that, far from teaching the same thing, the major religions have radically different perspectives on the religious ultimate."

—HAROLD A. NETLAND[6]

Sharing Our Stories

John's Story

Before I turned 25, I had traveled across Africa, the Middle East, Asia, Latin America, and Europe with my dad. We were invited by Christians in different countries to talk to the locals and present the uniqueness of Jesus Christ. I often spoke to students in schools and universities. My dad and I addressed larger audiences in stadiums, auditoriums, and outdoor venues. On some occasions I lived with families that held to one of the different religious views presented in this book. I also visited their shrines and holy places.

I first traveled to Africa when I was 18. Then, *Time* magazine had characterized Ethiopia as one of the ten places in the world untouched by civilization. I could see why on the day I left Addis Ababa—I flew on a little DC-3 that had chickens and goats running up and down the aisle of the airplane. We flew for about two hours and landed in a valley surrounded by huge mountains. There were no houses or buildings, no cars or people, nor even an airport. We landed on a dusty grass runway in the quiet of the wilderness. Then the plane flew off, leaving me alone in the middle of nowhere.

Some time later a young man arrived on a small motorcycle and picked me up. We started off in a direction where there were no discernible roads that I could see, and eventually came upon some round huts made from dung and mud. One building was square and had an aluminum roof. It was where I would sleep that night, in an area known as the Wallamo territory.

The Wallamos were a fierce tribe who revered their tribal chiefs and powerful shamans. Their religion was animism—they believed in and worshipped the spirits that pervaded nature. I had come here on research in connection with my university studies in anthropology. The main question I wanted to answer was, "How would people who had never heard of Jesus or Christianity react once they heard and were left to themselves?" In 1928, nine missionaries had ridden 200 miles inland on mules over mountains and rivers to approach the Wallamo tribe. By 1935, only 17 Wallamos had become Christians.

When Italy invaded Ethiopia in 1935, the American and British embassies advised all their citizens to leave immediately. Ten missionaries felt led of God to stay. In the following months, when chaos broke out in the country, two of the missionaries were caught, mutilated, and murdered by tribe members. The other eight missionaries all lived in one house and wondered if they would be killed by hostile Wallamos, by retreating Ethiopian soldiers who were pillaging the land, or by Mussolini's advancing troops. The small number of Wallamo Christians, left to themselves, watched these missionaries experience starvation, persecution, and death. By 1937, this small group of Wallamo Christians had grown to 48. At that time, all the remaining missionaries were forced to evacuate Ethiopia.

As soon as the missionaries were gone, the 48 Wallamo Christians were captured by the Italian army and put into stockades. Every Christian was beaten with bull whips, most receiving 100 lashes, and some receiving four times that number. They were given no food or medical help, and at night they were left unprotected from the freezing winds. Members of the tribe watched as these Christians suffered and some died. The imprisoned Christians made up their own songs, and worshipped Christ while in stockades.

When they were finally released, they fearlessly testified about why they were willing to suffer for Christ. They explained the gospel—that God's son had come to earth to pay for all our sins by his death on the cross. This son then conquered death, sin, and Satan by rising from the dead. He now invited anyone from any nation to believe on him and promised he would forgive their sins, walk with them through life, and take them to heaven when they died.

When the missionaries left in 1937, there were only 48 native Christians. But when they returned five years later, astonishingly, there were 10,000 Christians and 100 churches. During that time, the only portion of Scripture the Wallamo Christians had was the Gospel of Mark, along with a pamphlet containing a small number of other verses. They made up their own hymns and built round church buildings that contained no furniture. As in other buildings in their culture, everyone sat on dirt floors.

The night I stayed in Wallamo territory, I met three of the leaders who had come to Christ in the 1930s, lived through the persecutions, and established churches. Their churches had sent out Christians to bring the gospel to other tribes—all without any missionary supervision. As they told their stories, they showed me the scars on their backs and legs where they had been whipped and beaten. This is just one of many amazing testimonies I've heard that have demonstrated to me the power of the gospel and the reality of Christ in the lives of people who were formerly in other religions.

A few years later, while traveling west of Nairobi, Kenya, I was informed we were entering a village in which the people had never heard of Christianity or the gospel of Jesus Christ. We stopped and ate with the people and asked if they would let us address them as a group. They agreed. As I waited, I couldn't help but wonder if they would be open to hearing about Jesus. How could I convey to them that Jesus was both God and man, had lived on this earth, and had the power and willingness to forgive and love them and enter their lives? Talking through interpreters, I learned that these people intuitively knew there was a great Creator God by looking at the star-filled sky at night. Even though they worshipped the evil spirits around them, they believed in the existence of a great spirit who was good—they just didn't know him. When I told them the great Creator had entered his creation as a man to die for their wicked ways and was willing to forgive them, be their friend, and give them power over the evil spirits, I found many of them very willing to enter into a personal relationship with Jesus Christ.

Some time later, while in Bangkok, Thailand, I stood at the entrance to a Shinto temple and watched people placing food and money before huge stone idols. The people would pray and light candles to the spirits and gods, and lie prostrate before them. I couldn't help but ask, "From where did their beliefs originate? Why should anyone believe they are true?"

On university campuses, I found many who were raised in Buddhism, Shintoism, and Hinduism who were eager to learn about the person of Jesus Christ and his power in this life and the next. In the Muslim islands of Indonesia and in the nations of North Africa, I have found those steeped in Islam who were curious about why Christians worship Jesus. How does he compare to Mohammad as a moral example? Was he more than a prophet? Did he really die on a cross?

On our television program I have talked with both practicing and former leaders of various world religions and movements. I have invited world-famous atheists such as Dr. Antony Flew and Dr. Paul Kurtz to debate Christian scholars. The questions in this book are among the most important ones that people of other persuasions have asked me. "Who is God? Who is Jesus? What is your authority, and why should we believe in Christianity? How does Christianity compare with our beliefs?"

All over the world I have found that people recognize not all religions are the same. And once they start to compare, they discover that Jesus Christ is absolutely unique. Further, there is solid historical evidence that supports the biblical accounts of Jesus' life, his claims, and his resurrection from the dead. Christianity does not ask a person to take a leap of blind faith. In the course of speaking to people who hold to different religious views, I have learned why they come to see Christianity as good news when they hear it. And I am glad you are willing to investigate the big deal about other religions as they relate to Jesus.

Doesn't Being Sincere Count?

Some people think it doesn't matter what you believe as long as you're sincere. Centuries ago, people sincerely believed that thunder was caused by gods at war. We now know that their sincere beliefs were grounded in superstition. People can be very sincere in what they believe, but they can also be sincerely wrong. While I (John) was in college, I was told of a student who took LSD and said he believed he could fly. He stepped off the edge of a ten-story building, but his beliefs didn't keep him from falling to his death.

I'm always amazed at how people so often say that sincerity is all you need when it comes to religion, but not to other parts of life. You'd never apply the "sincerity test" to a historical event such as World War II. You may sincerely believe that Hitler actually won, but you'd be wrong. And what about mathematics? No one in his right mind would say that if he sincerely believed hard enough, one plus one would equal three. Why think this way when it comes to spiritual issues?[7]

Dillon's Story

I grew up under the influences of a mother from a legalistic, Charismatic Christian background and a father from a near-nonexistent spiritual background. You could describe my start as a mixture of values for self-reliant hard work along with spiritual traditions consisting of countless do's and don'ts. Early on, however, my father experienced Jesus in a genuine way that sparked serious life-change. We began attending church regularly, prayed at dinner, and read from Luke 2 each Christmas morning.

Our church experience, for the most part, involved a small Baptist church that carried on the traditions of singing hymns, wearing suits, and saying prayers in King James language. The people were nice, but as a child, I felt like I entered a different world on Sunday mornings—one that was much older and more sacred than my everyday experience.

By the time I was on my own, my personal journey had already included a period of brief rebellion, return, and renewal. In short, I had quit attending church, saw the consequences of life apart from spiritual direction, and turned to the Jesus of Scripture—all in less than a year. This time my life centered not on a religion, but a relationship that, in a highly personal and supernatural way, changed my daily thoughts and actions. I began to read the Bible, discovering words of life that have altered my way of living ever since.

"It is highly misleading to speak as if all religions share a common soteriological goal [salvation] and simply differ on the means to reach it."[8]

More than 14 years later, I'm still following the practices I began during those early times of meditation and study. My quest is not complete by any means. Even a master's degree in theology, several years of research in religion, and teaching the Bible to others have not closed my mind to further investigation into spiritual truth. However, I have seen that our culture is riddled with broken lives, destroyed relationships, and devastated family situations. My life stands far from perfect, but I live in peace and with purpose as I continue to allow Jesus to live in and through my life.

My hope for you as we share this spiritual conversation is twofold. For those deeply steeped in their religious beliefs, I hope to open your worldview to include a better understanding of the millions of others who hold to different beliefs. If you've lived as a Christian all of your life, for instance, it's extremely difficult to empathize with someone who has grown up Muslim or agnostic because you've never experienced it. What you read in these pages can help as you continue to build bridges with others and communicate your own faith.

Second, I desire to help those who seek truth to ask the tough questions and search for the answers to crucial spiritual matters. Whether you believe nothing about God or have lived a lifetime within a tradition of another type—Catholic, Mormon, Hindu, or otherwise—there is more to learn that I hope will lead to a life of positive change and ultimately a growing relationship with Jesus as the Christ.

As a full-time writer, I sometimes do my work at Starbucks, jotting down thoughts or doing online research at a table next to groups talking about their families, sharing business presentations, or even studying the Bible. One advantage to my virtual office location is that I am able to imagine one of those people sharing this conversation with me: "What are your thoughts on other religions? What do you believe happens to a person after death? How do your spiritual beliefs impact your life? What do you believe about Jesus?"

These questions and how you answer them are not simply academic issues. They represent some of the most significant matters in life. We are glad to have you join us for this journey to discuss the big deal about other religions.

Part One: | # Christianity and Roman Catholicism

t's been estimated that some 2.1 billion people belong to some form of Christianity. This represents approximately one out of every three people on the planet. Yet today's Christianity often suffers from a lack of clarity regarding what it means to be a Christian—what Christians believe, and who is one and who isn't. Many of today's studies include Protestants, Roman Catholics, members of the Eastern Orthodox Church, Latter-day Saints, Jehovah's Witnesses, and other such groups as being in the same category. This, however, is not accurate. That's why it is important not only to discuss Christianity but to *define* what it is, understand its various historical expressions (such as Roman Catholicism), and reaffirm what defines biblical Christianity.

In our discussion together, we'll first review biblical Christianity and its beliefs on the major issues of faith. We'll use this Bible-based worldview as our basis of comparison with the other groups we investigate in this book.

Second, we'll take a look at the unique characteristics of Roman Catholicism. With nearly one billion members in various churches worldwide, its historical influence and continuing numerical significance is unparalleled. Yet much disagreement exists as to its beliefs in comparison with biblical Christianity. Beliefs about Roman Catholicism's emphasis on the authority of the pope and upon tradition, along with its views of Mary and several other distinctions, have served as sources of controversy for centuries. Together we'll ask tough questions about these issues and see what the Bible teaches about them.

Are you ready to discover the big deal about other religions? Let's begin with the foundation that will serve as the basis of our study—biblical Christianity.

Christianity:

What's the Big Deal About Jesus?

1

"Christianity is good for you, but it's not right for me. I think you ought to believe whatever makes you happy and gives you peace."

"Christianity is the 'right' religion—isn't that being naive?"

The label *Christianity* covers a broad range of people today. While over 2.1 billion people are statistically considered followers of Jesus Christ, polls by religious researcher George Barna have observed that only four percent of American Christians hold to a biblical worldview (that is, beliefs consistent with the Bible's teachings), and just 51 percent of Christian clergy hold to such a view.[1] As a result, even many who call themselves Christians have agreed with the quotes that appear above, asking if it is perhaps naïve to claim Christianity is the only way to God.

However, the above quotes are inconsistent with Christianity's origins and founder. In this chapter we'll briefly review how Christianity began, consider its early beliefs, introduce its founder, and investigate the reliability of the New Testament, which is part of the Bible.

A Firm Foundation

All of Christianity is built around one basic belief: the resurrection of its founder, Jesus of Nazareth. On Passover Friday around A.D. 30, Jesus was executed on a Roman cross on the accusation of conspiracy against the government. The Sanhedrin (Jewish leaders) had insisted that the Roman leader Pilate condemn Jesus, though Pilate had not found him guilty of any crimes worthy of death. After the crucifixion, death, and burial of Jesus in a tomb, the body disappeared three days later. Immediately this was followed by many "Jesus sightings" reported over the next 40 days. A social revolution began ten days later in Jerusalem, Israel, as over 3000 people joined the movement after a street message given by the apostle Peter (Acts 2). Christianity was off and running, and has been growing ever since.

Oxford University theologian Dr. Alister McGrath has noted,

> The identity of Christianity is inextricably linked with the uniqueness of Christ, which is in turn grounded in the Resurrection and Incarnation.[2]

How do we know Jesus came back to life? First, the 27 books of the New Testament are based upon this one event—the resurrection of Jesus. Despite the attacks of many, the writings of Christianity have been shown to have emerged during the first century with the courageous message that Jesus, a man executed by the government, was alive. This carried many implications about his life and death and beyond. What other motive did these writers have except that they truly believed all this had occurred?

In addition, many individuals of that day claimed to have encountered Jesus after his death. According to the Gospel writers and the missionary Paul, Jesus appeared a total of at least 12 times after his return from death:

The Post-Resurrection Appearances of Jesus Christ

#	Sighting	Source
1	Mary Magdalene	Mark 16:9; John 20:11-18
2	Women returning from the tomb	Matthew 28:9-10
3	Two men walking to Emmaus	Mark 16:12-13; Luke 24:13-32
4	Peter	Luke 24:34; 1 Corinthians 15:5
5	10 disciples; two men from Emmaus	Luke 24:36-43; John 20:19-23
6	11 disciples (including Thomas)	John 20:24-29
7	7 disciples	John 21:1-24
8	500 people at one time	1 Corinthians 15:6
9	James, the half-brother of Jesus	1 Corinthians 15:7
10	11 disciples	Matthew 28:16-20
11	11 disciples before Jesus returned to heaven	Luke 24:50-53
12	Paul	Acts 9:3-6; 1 Corinthians 15:8

In just one of these sightings, over 500 people claimed to see Jesus alive after his death. Did you know that if each of those 500 people were to testify in court for only six minutes, including time for cross-examination, we would have an amazing 50 hours of first-hand testimony? Few other events from over 2000 years ago find this level of support. None offer the number of witnesses the resurrection does for a *supernatural* event.

Further, the changed lives of the early followers of Jesus supported their report that Jesus was alive. All but one of Jesus' 11 followers died for his belief in the resurrection of Jesus. Hundreds—if not thousands—of other Christians suffered or died within the first century of Christianity for their beliefs as well. The killing of the first Christian martyr, Stephen, led to the persecution of the Jerusalem church, which eventually forced many Christians to flee the area for safety.

"Could you convince thousands of people in our own day that President Kennedy had resurrected from the dead? There's no way...unless it really happened."[3]

The amazing phenomenon of Christianity's growth also stands as a powerful testimony that this faith is based on a supernatural resurrection. How could a crucified Jew (Jesus), former tax collector (Matthew), Jesus-hater (Paul), and small town fishermen (including Peter) establish a movement that has resulted in the largest religion on Earth? How could this happen?

When Christianity began, the Roman Empire was the greatest government of the time. Yet 300 years later, the Roman Empire had crumbled, and Christianity was continuing to grow. This, in spite of its humble beginning as a grassroots network of individuals who witnessed that Jesus had come back to life. Even though the proclamation of Jesus' teachings produced persecution of the greatest kind, Christianity continued to spread across the Roman Empire—all the way to the palace of Caesar in Rome, the world's political and social capital.[4]

Christianity 101

So Christianity originated from a group of Jesus-followers who spread the message that they had personally witnessed his three years of teaching and miracles, watched him die on a cross, and then personally met, saw, talked to, ate with, and received instructions from him after his resurrection from the dead. But what are the *core beliefs* of Christianity? There are six central elements of traditional Christianity.

First, there is the common understanding of Jews and Christians that there is only one true God—who is infinite, holy, loving, just, and true. In addition, Christians believe that in the nature (presence) of the one true God there exists three persons—Father, Son, and Holy Spirit. Christianity does not believe in three gods, but one. As Dr. Norman Geisler, bestselling author and cofounder of Southern Evangelical Seminary, has written,

The Trinity is not the belief that God is three personas and only one person at the same time and in the same sense. That would be a contradiction. Rather, it is the belief that there are three persons in one nature. This may be a mystery, but it is not a contradiction. That is, it may go beyond reason's ability to comprehend completely, but it does not go against reason's ability to apprehend consistently.

Further, the Trinity is not the belief that there are three natures in one nature or three essences in one essence. That would be a contradiction. Rather, Christians affirm that there are three persons in one essence...He is one in the sense of his essence but many in the sense of his persons. So there is no violation of the law of non-contradiction in the doctrine of the Trinity.[5]

Traditional Christianity also accepts the 66 books of the Holy Bible as revelation from God, perfect and authoritative for all spiritual matters. While Roman Catholicism accepts the additional authority of the pope and church tradition, and Eastern Orthodoxy accepts church tradition as equal in authority to the Bible, the earliest traditional Christianity and later Protestant Christianity[6] have been based solely on God's written revelation through his apostles and prophets.

Third, Christians believe every person who has ever lived (with the exception of Jesus Christ) has been born a sinner separated from God. It is our sin nature that keeps us from knowing and experiencing God and creates a need for reconciliation through a means only God can provide.

Fourth, in his infinite love, God has provided the solution to the barrier between himself and humanity through Jesus Christ. The Bible teaches that the death of Jesus provides payment for our sins, and on the basis of our believing, he is our sinbearer and he will forgive us the moment we believe. All this is confirmed by Jesus' resurrection from the dead—he has paid the penalty for sin and conquered death. In this way God offers a basis for a person to place his or her faith in Christ and to enter into a personal relationship with Jesus, in which he enters your life and you walk through life with his power and guidance.

Fifth, this rescue or salvation God offers through Jesus is based solely on *what God has done* rather than on *what people do*. In other words, salvation is a free gift based on God's grace to us (unearned favor) rather than good works or deeds we can accomplish, though these will accompany a person once he or she becomes a Christian. One of the major points of contention during the Protestant Reformation resulted from the Roman Catholic Church's unbiblical teaching that God's grace consists of humans cooperating with God's grace to merit salvation, rather than receiving salvation in full as a gift on the basis of faith alone the moment a person believes.

Sixth, Christians believe in an eternal afterlife. God allows individuals the ability to choose or reject him, and after death, that decision is final. Those who have chosen to believe in Jesus will enjoy eternity with him in heaven, while those who decline will spend eternity in hell, separated from God. God will accept every person's decision and not force him or her to change their mind. While all this may sound politically incorrect in our culture, it has stood as an essential component of Christian teaching from the earliest times. The choice we make here on earth will have eternal consequences.

Jesus: Founder and CEO of Christianity

Christian philosopher Dr. C. Stephen Evans points out that "it is an essential part of Christian faith that Jesus is God in a unique and exclusive way. It follows from this that all religions [that disagree] cannot be equally true."[7] Again, if different religions teach contradictory things about who God is, salvation, the afterlife, and even Jesus, then one or another could be true, but they can't all be true at the same time. What are the big super-signs that help us decide which religion is true? According to biblical Christianity, if Jesus claimed to be God and proved his claim by his resurrection, then he is God and Christianity is true. No other religious leader in history has claimed to be God and risen from the dead.

Further, there are at least seven concepts Jesus taught about himself that stand unique to Christianity. First, Jesus communicated that he fulfilled biblical prophecy, given hundreds of years in advance, that he was the promised Messiah. He repeatedly claimed to be the person that God's Messiah was predicted to be, and many scholars have created extensive lists of these prophetic connections. Here are some examples of prophecies Jesus fulfilled:

Prophecy	Old Testament Prophecy	New Testament Fulfillment
Born of a virgin	Isaiah 7:14	Matthew 1:18,25
Born in Bethlehem	Micah 5:2	Matthew 2:1
Preceded by a messenger	Isaiah 40:3	Matthew 3:1-2
Rejected by his own people	Isaiah 53:3	John 7:5; 7:48
Betrayed by a close friend	Isaiah 41:9	John 13:26-30
His side pierced	Zechariah 12:10	John 19:34
His death by crucifixion	Psalm 22:1,11-18	Luke 23:33; John 19:23-24
His resurrection	Psalm 16:10	Acts 13:34-37

Second, Jesus stands as a unique, unparalleled individual among the leaders of various world religions. He made predictions about the future that could only be made by someone who claimed to be God. Further, he noted in advance several of the things that would occur at the time of his death and resurrection. Unlike anyone else, he also promised to one day return to earth to set up his future kingdom.

The Seven "I Ams" of Jesus in John's Gospel

- "I am the bread of life" (John 6:35,48; see also verse 51).
- "I am the light of the world" (John 8:12).
- "I am the gate for the sheep" (John 10:7; see also verse 9).

- "I am the good shepherd" (John 10:11,14).
- "I am the resurrection and the life" (John 11:25).
- "I am the way and the truth and the life" (John 14:6).
- "I am the true vine" (John 15:1; see also verse 5).

Further, Jesus is unique in his nature, being fully divine and fully human nature in one person. Jesus was born as a man without sin through a miraculous virgin birth. He challenged his own family, disciples, and even his enemies to prove him guilty of sin, but none could do so.[8] Think of the reaction you would receive if you asked your parents, brothers, sisters, and friends, "Can any of you point to *one* sin I have committed?" Those closest to us know our faults. We all have them. Yet Jesus lived a perfect life free of sin.

As God's divine son, Jesus performed miracles, healings, and exorcisms; fulfilled Jewish prophecies; and accomplished his own resurrection. In these ways he affirmed his divine nature, displaying power far beyond that of any person who has ever lived. Today people downplay the miracles, but they are documented in careful detail in the Bible, and even Jesus' enemies did not deny his miracles. They weren't able to. So they just claimed that he performed them with the help of evil powers (Matthew 12:24).

The Exorcisms of Jesus

Exorcism	Source
1. Healed a demon-possessed man at Capernaum	Mark 1:21-28; Luke 4:31-37
2. Drove out demons and evil spirits	Matthew 8:16-17; Mark 1:32-39; Luke 4:33-41
3. Healed the man possessed by demons at the Gadarenes	Matthew 8:28-34; Mark 5:1-20; Luke 8:26-39
4. Drove a demon out of a mute man, who then spoke	Matthew 9:32-34; Mark 3:20-22

Christianity is also the only major religion whose founder sacrificed his life for the sins of those who would choose to believe in him. Jesus' horrific death on the cross stood as proof of his statement that "the Son of Man [Jesus] did not come to be served, but to serve, and to give his life as a ransom for many."[9]

The Nature Miracles of Jesus

	The Miracle	Source
1.	Calming the wind and waves	Matthew 8:26; Mark 4:39; Luke 8:24
2.	Walking on water	Matthew 14:25; Mark 6:48; John 6:19
3.	Money in the fish's mouth	Matthew 17:27
4.	Withering of the fig tree	Matthew 21:19; Mark 11:14
5.	Miraculous catch of fish	Luke 5:4-7
6.	Turning water into wine	John 2:7-8
7.	Second miraculous catch of fish	John 21:6
8.	Feeding the 4000	Matthew 15:32-38; Mark 8:1-9
9.	Feeding the 5000	Matthew 14:13-21; Mark 6:34-44; Luke 9:12-17; John 6:5-12

Sixth, as mentioned earlier, Jesus also rose from the dead. Those in his time could never account for his empty tomb and the disappearance of his body. Jesus' followers spanned the known world testifying of his resurrection (his actual bodily appearing to them), teaching his words, and dying for their belief in him.

Finally, Jesus promises, at the end of time, to personally judge every person who ever lived. It would be eternally disappointing to have Jesus look at us, fairly judge us, and conclude, "I never knew you" (Matthew 7:23).

Christianity by the Book

Those who want to investigate the truthfulness of the original

Christian message can look to a wealth of manuscript evidence regarding the transmission of the 27 books of the New Testament through the years. The New Testament manuscripts offer more supporting evidence than any other ancient book. Christians also accept the Jewish scriptures (the Old Testament) as part of their holy book, the Bible. Traditional Christianity believes in the inerrancy of Scripture, meaning the original words of the Bible's books are without error and perfect in every way.[10]

As a result, Bible translation, distribution, and teaching stand as important responsibilities within Christianity. The Bible is the most translated book in history, has been used as the script for the most-watched film in history (the *Jesus* film), and has enjoyed greater distribution than any book in the world. Over 100 million copies of the New Testament or Bible are sold *every year* worldwide.

Interesting Statistics About the Bible

- The Bible was written over a period of 1600 years,
- by more than 40 authors of every sort—kings, peasants, fishermen, poets, shepherds, government officials, teachers, and prophets—
- in three languages (Hebrew, Aramaic, and Greek),
- on three continents—Asia, Africa, and Europe.[11]

What Makes Christianity Unique?

"Christianity isn't about people in search of God, but rather God in search of people."

—STEVE RUSSO[12]

Many have suggested that Christianity is about having a personal relationship with Jesus, and not performing good works and following rituals. Religious movements throughout history ultimately hold to a significantly different common thread—that certain actions or works are *required* to obtain a blissful afterlife. In Christianity, however, the key to reaching God here and now and dwelling with him for eternity is to receive and trust in a gift already provided by its founder, Jesus Christ. As the apostle Paul made clear to Christians at Ephesus, "God saved you by his grace when you believed. And you can't take credit for this; it is a gift from God. Salvation is not a reward for the good things we have done, so none of us can boast about it."[13]

God's gift of salvation also brings assurance. If Jesus' righteous life and atoning death on the cross is the sole basis for God's gift, then a Christian doesn't have to worry about earning or losing that gift. Once the gift is received, it belongs to the Christian forever because it rests on what Jesus did—not what the Christian did or does in the past, present, or future.

Christianity in Summary

As we compare and contrast the beliefs of various religions throughout this book, we hope to make the distinctives of each one as clear as possible. Here, we summarize the key teachings of Christianity:

Belief	Basic Description
God	One God in three persons—Father, Son, and Holy Spirit.
Holy Book	The 66 books of the Holy Bible are the authoritative works of Christianity.
Sin	All people have sinned (except Jesus).
Jesus Christ	God's perfect son, holy, resurrected, divine (second person of the Trinity) yet also fully human.
Salvation	Obtained only by God's grace through faith in Jesus Christ, not by human effort.
Afterlife	All people will enter heaven or hell upon death based on whether they have salvation in Jesus Christ. The Bible does not teach reincarnation, annihilation (ending of the soul), or the existence of purgatory.

Some people assume that biblical Christianity and Roman Catholicism are essentially similar. But is that the case? What differences exist? Are these differences really a big deal, or only minor details? Our next chapter will address these questions head-on.

The One True Church?

2

The Roman Catholic Church includes nearly one billion members around the world today, making it the largest segment of Christianity. Yet the Roman Catholic Church calls itself the one true church. What does this mean? In what ways is Roman Catholicism different from biblical Christianity? And should we be concerned about those differences?

In this chapter we'll discuss two major distinctions between biblical Christianity and Roman Catholicism—the issues of the pope's authority and the importance of sacred tradition—and consider several other differences that emerge from these two major distinctions. As we journey together, we'll find that though biblical Christianity and Roman Catholicism share a common origin and some overlapping beliefs, they are ultimately two separate faiths under the broad umbrella of Christianity.

The Role of Sacred Tradition

The Protestant reformers of the sixteenth and seventeenth centuries differed with the teachings of the church at Rome concerning the concept of *sola scriptura,* which is Latin for "Scripture alone." These reformers held that the Bible's teachings were the only source of authority regarding matters of the Christian faith. As a result, these reformers condemned many of the extrabiblical and antibiblical traditions that had developed in the Roman Catholic Church. While "only Scripture" became the basis behind the Protestant movement, the Roman Catholic Church voted to maintain its stance at the Council of Trent (1545–1563), officially stating that the Roman Catholic Church held the power to interpret what the Bible says.

At the second Vatican Council (1962–1965), the Catholic Church reaffirmed their claim. In summary, the Vatican Council argued that the apostles passed on their written letters, epistles, oral teachings, and their authority to the succeeding bishops, establishing a pattern of sacred tradition that includes additional teachings not found in the Bible. Because these traditions were passed down from supposed apostolic authority, they are considered of equal importance with the Bible itself. Rather than holding to the Bible as the sole authority in matters of faith, the Catholic Church holds to the authority of the Bible *plus* their developed traditions that grew as each subsequent generation of leaders added their own ideas.

The Role of the Pope's Authority

The Roman Catholic Church teaches that when the pope speaks *ex cathedra* (Latin for "from his chair"), he is infallible and without mistake in matters of faith and morals. Papal infallibility was officially defined and put forth on July 18, 1870 at the First Vatican Council. This means the Roman Catholic Church did not officially hold to the position of papal infallibility for the first 1800 years of Christianity's existence. A thorough discussion of the Vatican I council that approved this teaching can be found in August Hasler's book entitled *How the Pope Became Infallible*. A former Vatican secretary who had access to the Vatican's library archives, he studied documents unavailable to other scholars. His assessment on the issue of the pope's authority noted:

> It has become increasingly obvious, in fact, that the dogma
> of papal infallibility has no basis either in the Bible or

the history of the Church during the first millennium. If, however, the First Vatican Council was not free, then neither was it ecumenical. And in that case its decrees have no claim to validity. So the way is clear to revise this Council and, at the same time, to escape from a situation which both history and theology find more and more indefensible. Is this asking too much of the Church? Can it ever admit that a council erred, that in 1870 Vatican I made the wrong decision?[1]

The decree regarding the pope's infallibility has been controversial from the start. It states that the pope is unable to make a mistake when speaking from his chair of authority. This contrasts with what we see in the lives of the most preeminent church leaders in the Bible. Peter, the lead apostle of Jesus, denied Jesus three times on the night of his arrest (Luke 22:54-62). The apostle Paul, even long after his conversion, shared that he continued to struggle with sin (Romans 7:7-25). If the top leaders of the early church were fallible, how can anyone say that the pope is infallible?

Roman Catholic Traditions That Conflict with the Bible

Of the many other differences found between Roman Catholicism and Protestantism, we will present four of major significance. These include teachings about salvation (how a person comes to know God and reach heaven), the issue of purgatory, the definitions of venial and mortal sins, and the role of Mary, the mother of Jesus.

Salvation by Faith and Works

According to the *Catechism of the Catholic Church*, "From the time of the apostles, becoming a Christian has been accomplished by a journey and initiation in several stages."[2] Roman Catholicism teaches that salvation, or establishing a personal relationship with God that leads to life in heaven, is based on both faith *and* a series of good works. These works include what are known as the seven sacraments:

1. Baptism

The *Catechism of the Catholic Church* states:

> By baptism, all sins are forgiven, original sin and all personal sins, as well as all punishment for sin.[3]
>
> Holy baptism is the basis of the whole Christian life, the gateway to life is the Spirit, and the door which gives access to the other sacraments.[4]
>
> Baptism is necessary for salvation for those to whom the gospel has been proclaimed and who have had the possibility of asking for this sacrament.[5]
>
> For the baptized, children or adults, faith must grow after baptism.[6]
>
> Baptism...is the beginning of new life.[7]

For infants or adults, baptism supposedly provides sanctifying grace and erases original sin. However, other works are required to keep this grace throughout life (the other six sacraments). In contrast, biblical Christianity believes baptism is simply an important public sign of a person's decision to follow Christ, and that it has nothing to do with salvation and forgiveness of sin, which occur only when a person puts his or her faith *in what Christ has done on the cross.* Ephesians 2:8-9 says, "It is by grace you have been saved, through faith—and this not from yourselves, it is the gift of God—not by works, so that no one can boast."

2. Confirmation

Children are confirmed at the age of 12 after a time of instruction in the church's beliefs. This sacrament is necessary for the completion of baptismal grace and provides a fuller outpouring of the Holy Spirit. "Confirmation brings an increase and deepening of baptismal grace,"[8] according to the *Catechism.* Biblical Christianity, by contrast, says a deeper knowledge of Scripture and obedience to the teachings of Christ draw the Christian into a closer walk with the Holy Spirit.

3. Holy Eucharist

> What material food produces in our bodily life, Holy Communion wonderfully achieves in our spiritual life.
>
> Communion...preserves, increases, and renews the life of grace received at baptism.[9]

In Roman Catholic churches, the Mass or Eucharist (also known as communion or the Lord's Supper) is shared by a priest and consists of elements that are said to miraculously become the blood and body of Christ when consecrated by the priest. As a result of participation in the Mass, a person receives further justifying grace with the hope that by the end of his lifetime, God will grant ultimate justification. But in biblical Christianity, communion is practiced as a remembrance of Christ's sacrifice for our sins, and is not viewed as part of a person's salvation (1 Corinthians 11:23-29).

4. Penance or Confession

Roman Catholicism teaches it is necessary for followers to confess their sins to a priest in order to be forgiven for sins committed after baptism. The Bible, however, teaches that we confess our sins to the Lord (1 John 1:9). The Roman Catholic teaching regarding penance states:

> Christ instituted the sacrament of penance for all sinful members of his church; above all for those who, since baptism, have fallen into grave sin, and have thus lost their baptismal grace and wounded ecclesial communion. It is to them that the sacrament of penance offers a new possibility to convert and to recover the grace of justification. The fathers of the church present this sacrament as "the second plank [of salvation] after the shipwreck which is the loss of grace."[10]

So the Roman Catholic Church teaches that after baptism, if a person commits a mortal sin, he loses his salvation. In order to regain salvation, the person must come via the sacrament of divine penance, which has three parts. The first part is *contrition*—a person must be sorry for his sins. Second, there must be *confession* of each mortal sin to a priest. Third, a person must do *works of satisfaction* such as fasting, saying prayers, almsgiving, or doing works of piety. Anyone who commits a mortal sin and does not do penance will not regain salvation and will not be forgiven by God. And forgiveness doesn't take effect until the works are completed.

Biblical Christianity teaches that once a person puts his faith in Christ, he is saved forever because Christ did all that was necessary to purchase the salvation (Romans 3:21-26). It all rests on him. If a person sins after believing in Christ, it affects his relationship with Christ, but not whether he will go to heaven.

5. Anointing of the Sick

This is a practice in which a priest prays over a sick or dying person and anoints him or her with oil, often oil blessed by a bishop. The *Catechism* states, "The anointing of the sick completes our conformity to the death and resurrection of Christ, just as baptism began it."[11] This practice is said to be based on James 5:14-15, which states:

> Is any one of you sick? He should call the elders of the church to pray over him and anoint him with oil in the name of the Lord. And the prayer offered in faith will make the sick person well; the Lord will raise him up.

However, the Bible does not present anointing as an additional element of a person's salvation. Biblically, the practice simply involves praying for a person who is sick to become well.

6. Holy Orders

This is considered an ordination for Catholic ministers, either as deacon, priest, or bishop. "Ordination...confers a gift of the Holy Spirit that permits the exercise of a sacred power,"[12] according to Catholic teaching. The Bible speaks of ordination for elders and deacons in the pastoral letters of the New Testament (1 Timothy 3:1-2; 2 Timothy 1:6; Titus 2:15). However, the biblical data does not suggest that a transfer of the Holy Spirit takes place during an ordination. Similar to the Old Testament practice of anointing kings with oil to set them apart as leaders, ordination is an act to show that a particular person has been selected and approved for church leadership.

7. Matrimony

Marriage is held in great esteem in the Roman Catholic Church. Divorce can cut a Catholic off from the benefits of the Eucharist.

These seven sacraments provide a series of "steps" or a process for individuals within the Roman Catholic Church to receive more and more justifying grace. In this way they strive up to the time of death, at which time it is hoped God will grant ultimate justification. Many of these seven practices *resemble* biblical traditions but are used in ways that teach that it is necessary for a person to participate in these practices in order to merit forgiveness and justifying grace. This is in direct contrast with the Bible, which says the person who comes to faith in Jesus Christ is forgiven of all sin based on faith in Christ's atoning death, and nothing more. Romans 6:23 summarizes Christian teaching on this issue by saying, "The wages of sin is death, but the gift of God is eternal life in Christ Jesus our Lord."

Purgatory

Unfortunately, even faithful Roman Catholics exit life uncertain about whether they will immediately enter heaven. Why? The Roman Catholic Church teaches that Christians who are guilty of venial sins first go to purgatory. They cannot go to heaven until they are fully purified. Not only are Christians purged of venial sins in purgatory, but they must also pay any temporal punishment still due from other sins. Roman Catholicism states that a person does not remain and suffer in purgatory forever, as a person does in hell. Rather, after a person's soul is cleansed of imperfections, he then enters heaven. *The Catholic Encyclopedia* notes:

> The souls of those who have died in the state of grace suffer for a time a purging that prepares them to enter heaven... The purpose of purgatory is to cleanse one of imperfections, venial sins, and faults, and to remit or do away with the temporal punishment due to mortal sins that have been forgiven in the Sacrament of Penance. It is an intermediate state in which the departed souls can atone for unforgiven sins before receiving their final reward.[13]

Biblical Christianity strongly denies the doctrine of purgatory. Scripture teaches that there is only a heaven and a hell. Further, it is an affront to the grace of God to teach that Christ forgives only part of the penalty for sin, and there still remains some penalty that the person who sins needs to pay. If a person must pay for even the temporal punishment of his sins, then Jesus didn't really pay it all at the cross. The Bible clearly proclaims:

> The blood of Jesus, his son, purifies us from *all sin* (1 John 1:7).

> By one sacrifice he has made perfect forever those who are being made holy (Hebrews 10:14).

> My dear children, I write this to you so that you will not sin. But if anybody does sin, we have one who speaks to the Father in our defense—Jesus Christ, the Righteous One. He is the atoning sacrifice for our sins, and not only for ours but also for the sins of the whole world (1 John 2:1-2).

Yet purgatory is defined in Roman Catholicism as a place of both joy and suffering, a paradox that fits the biblical descriptions of neither heaven nor hell. Those in purgatory cannot help themselves, according to Catholic teaching, but those on Earth can pray for them, offer Mass for them, and even seek indulgences on behalf of the dead.

What are indulgences? Indulgences are acts Catholics can carry out to help those in purgatory reach heaven more quickly. These acts include prayers and good deeds. This justification for indulgences is supposedly based on the teaching Jesus gave to the apostle Peter regarding the ability to bind and loose sins (Matthew 16:19). But this authority to bind or loose sins was simply the privilege and responsibility of all the apostles and early Christian leaders to proclaim that anyone who confessed their sins to Jesus and believed in his power could be assured God had forgiven him. Roman Catholicism, however, teaches that followers can intervene through prayer and good works.

There are two types of indulgences: partial or plenary (complete). Plenary indulgences can be granted only by the pope, and they cover all sins of the deceased person. As such, plenary indulgences are a rare occurrence. More commonly, partial indulgences are granted. These can be given by bishops, archbishops, or cardinals. Typically, partial indulgences reduce, by a certain amount of time, the duration of a person's stay in purgatory. For instance, a partial indulgence of six months would indicate that the bishop (or other leader) has granted the deceased person six fewer months of time in purgatory before entering heaven (of course, no one knows the total length of time any person has to stay in purgatory, so there is much uncertainty in this system).

Venial and Mortal Sins

In a debate I (John) moderated several years ago between Father Mitchell Pacwa and Dr. Walter Martin, we discussed the role of justification (being made right with God) as presented by both Roman Catholics and Protestants. Father Pacwa stated that, according to Roman Catholic teaching, there is "a distinction of different kinds of sin. If one commits serious sin [mortal sins], one can cut oneself off from Christ and thereby lose one's justification." He was presenting the commonly held view of Roman Catholicism regarding venial and mortal sins.

I shared with my television audience in that same program that "Catholicism believes that justification can be destroyed; that is, justifying grace within a man can be obliterated by his committing mortal sin (such as not attending Mass). Roman Catholicism distinguishes between *venial* sins—sins that are not so serious that they involve the destruction of justifying grace—and *mortal* sins, which are sins so serious that the grace of justification can then be destroyed within man. If a man commits mortal sin and destroys his justification, Catholicism teaches it can be regained only via the Sacrament of Penance, which involves confession, absolution, and satisfaction.

> Catholics *do* believe in Christ but are reminded that their justification also depends on their works cooperating with Christ. A man cannot know his own heart, so being subject to many temptations, he may commit a variety of mortal sins, any one of which could destroy his justification. That is why the Council of Trent stated, "Each one, when he regards himself and his own weakness and indisposition, may have fear and apprehension touching his own grace; seeing that no one can know with a certainty of faith, which cannot be subject to error, that he has obtained the grace of God." So for Catholicism, a man can lose his justification and can't be sure he will someday be in heaven.[14]

Even a lifelong, faithful Catholic who commits a mortal sin shortly before death and does not repent via penance will go to hell forever with no chance of getting out.

The Roman Catholic View of Sin

Venial Sins   Venial sins are slight offenses against the law of God in matters of less importance. Or, in matters of great importance, it is an offense committed without sufficient reflection or full consent of the will. Venial sin weakens the individual but it does not deprive him of spiritual life. There is no obligation to confess venial sins, which can be remitted through penance, attending Mass, and purgatory.

Mortal Sins   Mortal sins are grievous offenses against the law of God.
They are called mortal because they kill or deprive one of
spiritual life and bring everlasting death and damnation on
the soul.

Adapted from justforcatholics.org

Biblical Christianity teaches that *all* sins are mortal and separate us from God. But the moment a person believes in Jesus' work on the cross as payment for his or her sins, he or she is immediately forgiven all sins—past, present, and future. However, Christians do commit sins after salvation. These sins affect their *relationship* with God, but they don't deprive them of God's gift of eternity with him in heaven. While different sins result in varying consequences in this life, all sin is offensive to God, who is holy.

The Role of Mary, Mother of Jesus

In Luke 1:28, Mary is called highly favored and blessed among women. Based on this verse, Roman Catholics have given special honor to Mary—and over the centuries, this honor has evolved to the point that Mary has been worshipped and is prayed to.

Roman Catholics attempt to define their adoration of Mary as being different than their worship of Jesus. According to Catholic dogma, there are three levels of worship. The first level, *latria,* has to do with the worship of God. The second level, *dulia,* relates to the veneration of angels and recognized saints of the church. The third level, *hyperdulia,* is reserved only for Mary, who receives a higher level of veneration than other saints. However, the Bible indicates that only God is to be worshipped, and condemns the worship of angels or people (Revelation 19:10; 22:8-9).

Another Catholic tradition that contradicts biblical teaching is the belief that Mary was conceived without sin, lived a sinless life, and had no other children after she gave birth to Jesus. This is called the teaching of the immaculate conception. However, the Bible teaches that everyone is born into sin, has sinned (Romans 3:23), and that

Mary had other children (Matthew 13:55; Mark 3:31-35), including James and Jude, the brothers of Jesus, who each wrote a book of the New Testament. In 1950, Pope Pius XII also proclaimed the Assumption of Mary as official church teaching, an unbiblical view that claims Mary's body and soul were taken directly to heaven.

Band of Brothers

Coming to his hometown, he began teaching the people in their synagogue, and they were amazed. "Where did this man get this wisdom and these miraculous powers?" they asked. "Isn't this the carpenter's son? Isn't his mother's name Mary, and aren't his brothers James, Joseph, Simon and Judas? Aren't all his sisters with us? Where then did this man get all these things?" (Matthew 13:54-56; see also Mark 6:3).

According to Matthew, one of Jesus' 12 disciples, Jesus had at least four brothers and two or more sisters ("sisters" is plural here). Roman Catholic teaching attempts to define these family members as extended family, such as cousins, but a normal reading of these verses indicates these were his siblings, especially in light of Mark 3:31-35, which speaks of Jesus' mother, brothers, and sisters coming to him. James and Judas (Jude) would later write New Testament books, and James was the leader of the Jerusalem church (see Acts 15).

Roman Catholics and Protestants in Dialogue

Toward the end of the twentieth century, Roman Catholic and Protestant leaders met frequently to discuss the similarities and differences between the two groups. In 1994, a significant document, "Evangelicals and Catholics Together: The Christian Commission in the Third Millennium," was released. In 1997 a document was released by some of the same participants, called "The Gift of Salvation." This attempted to address commonalities on this issue.

However, these documents have greatly overstated the agreements between these two systems of belief. Unfortunately, important areas of disagreement were neglected and some portions of the documents lacked in clarity.

Biblical Christianity Compared with Roman Catholicism

As we place classic Roman Catholic teachings alongside those of biblical Christianity, we find the following:

Topic	Roman Catholic Perspective	Biblical Perspective
God	One God in three persons, though angels, saints, and Mary are also highly revered.	One God in three persons— Father, Son, and Holy Spirit.
Holy Book	Accept the 66 books of the Bible as authoritative, along with additional books (the Apocrypha), Sacred Tradition, and papal infallibility.	The 66 books of the Holy Bible are the sole authoritative work for Christianity.
Sin	All people have sinned (except Jesus and his mother Mary). Also teaches that there are venial and mortal sins.	All people have sinned (except Jesus).
Jesus Christ	God's perfect son, resurrected, holy, divine (second person of the Trinity), yet also fully human.	God's perfect son, holy, resurrected, divine (second person of the Trinity), yet also fully human.
Salvation	Justification is obtained by doing meritorious works that cooperate with God's grace, with focus upon the seven sacraments.	Justification is obtained only by God's grace through faith in Jesus Christ, not by human effort or a result of cooperating with God's grace.
Afterlife	All souls enter either heaven, hell, or purgatory upon death. The prayers and deeds of living Catholics can help those in purgatory to reach heaven more quickly.	All people will enter either heaven or hell upon death, depending on whether they have salvation in Jesus Christ. The Bible does not mention purgatory.

Because of the vast differences that exist in the foundational beliefs of Roman Catholicism and biblical Christianity, we conclude that though some Catholics may believe differently than their church and are true Christians, Roman Catholicism as a religious system is not the same as biblical Christianity.

Why does this matter? Those who are biblical Christians need to know that when they talk with Roman Catholics, even though both may use many of the same words, those words have very different meanings. Defining grace, how a person receives salvation, and the views regarding the Bible, Mary, and the afterlife are all areas in which traditional Roman Catholics and biblical Christians will disagree significantly.

We want to transition now to the other major one-God religions that influence our world. While these groups worship one God, like Christians, they are different in many other ways. Are their differences really a big deal or not? Let's find out.

Part Two: Other One-God Religions

According to statistics, the three major monotheistic (one-God) religions—Christianity, Judaism, and Islam—comprise nearly 4.5 billion of the world's six billion people.[1] As we continue our conversation about what other religions believe and practice, we'll discuss the other two religions out of the "big three" that, along with Christianity, include nearly three out of every four people on the planet.

First, we'll discuss the unique beliefs of Judaism. It precedes both Christianity and Islam and claims to be the world's oldest religion. The Jewish people have endured the most horrific suffering, yet they continue to flourish in Israel and around the world. How did Judaism begin? What does it teach? Who was its founder? How reliable are its sacred writings? How does it compare to biblical Christianity?

Then our journey will transition to an investigation of modern Islam. What do Muslims believe? How did the Qur'an develop? How is Islam related to Judaism and Christianity? What is known about Islam's founder?

Along the way, you may want to write your own questions in the margins, circle important quotes, or journal some of your thoughts. (Also, don't forget you can e-mail us with your questions.) So get a pen, grab a cup of hot coffee, and settle down with a favorite snack as we learn about Judaism and Islam.

Why Do Jews Get to Be God's Chosen People?

3

"Jews are like everybody else, only more so."

—HOWLAND SPENCER[1]

oday, over 14 million people worldwide claim Jewish heritage.[2] However, many of us know of Judaism only from prominent individuals such as Albert Einstein or Steven Spielberg, or through films such as *Schindler's List* or bestselling books such as Elie Wiesel's *Night*. When it comes to what today's Jews believe or practice, many of us know very little.

While Judaism shares many historical similarities with Christianity, it certainly holds many distinctions as well. In our time together in this chapter, we'll take a look at how Judaism began, how it is defined today, what Jews believe, Jewish persecutions, and Judaism's connection with Christianity.

In the Beginning...

The LORD had said to Abram, "Leave your country, your people and your father's household and go to the land I will show you. I will make you into a great nation and I will bless you; I will make your name great, and you will be a blessing. I will bless those who bless you, and whoever curses you I will curse; and all peoples on earth will be blessed through you" (Genesis 12:1-3).

Long before Christianity and Islam came on the scene, Judaism's journey began through the ancient narrative of Abram, in which God promised Abram, "I will make you into a great nation." Later, Abram's name was changed to Abraham. Genesis records his calling to a new land, where God would bless him and make his name great.

The Jewish story continues through Isaac and Jacob, Jacob's 12 sons (who became the leaders of Israel's 12 tribes), Moses (who led Israel out of Egypt), generations of judges and kings, times of conquest from outside nations, and Jewish migration to many nations around the world.

"Judaism is the religion of the Jews. It was the first great faith to believe in one God."[3] Its fundamental beliefs are based on the words of Moses, which are recorded in the Torah, and on later interpretations of the Torah, which were written by Jewish religious leaders over subsequent centuries.

Did You Know...

...that more Jews live in the United States than in Israel? According to the *American Jewish Year Book,* 5.28 million Jews live in America, and 5.237 million Jews live in Israel. Other nations with substantial Jewish populations include France, Canada, the United Kingdom, Russia, and Argentina.[4]

Defining Judaism

At its most foundational level, Judaism is simply the religion of the Jews. However, when asked, What is a Jew? the answer can be much more complex. According to the Jewish perspective, we find that a Jew can be defined with the help of five key questions:[5]

Is Judaism a Religion?

In some ways, this question can easily be answered with a yes, but not by everyone. While outsiders may easily label all Jews as followers of Judaism, it is important to realize that some Jews consider themselves members of other religions, agnostics, or even atheists. Judaism is a religion, but is more than just a religion.

Are Jews a Race?

Some would argue that Jews are people of the same genetic background rather than a religion. From a Jewish perspective, genealogy is of great importance, but is not the only factor that makes a person a Jew. After all, even those who do not come from a Jewish genetic background can convert to Judaism. So Jews are more than simply an ethnic group.

Is Judaism a Culture?

Others suggest that Judaism is a culture based on its shared community practices and distinctives. Common holidays, certain foods, and shared language are the highlighted components of those with this viewpoint. However, to suggest Judaism is only a culture neglects its spiritual dimension. According to Jewish beliefs, Judaism exists because of God's calling to their forefather Abraham. Jewish people certainly share a common culture, but Jewish tradition makes Judaism far more than that.

Are Jews a Nation?

In 1948, Israel once again became identified as a nation. As a result, some people think of Jews as a nation of people. However, more Jews today live in the United States than in Israel. In addition, millions of Jews live in other nations all throughout the world and are not limited to one geographic region. While the ancient Jewish Scriptures speak of the Jewish nation, today's definition of *nation* blurs the comprehensive definition of Jews—a definition that includes God's promises in addition to a national identity.

Are Jews a Family?

Rabbi Adin Steinsaltz has suggested thinking of the Jewish people as being analogous to a family.[6] Throughout the Bible and Jewish literature, the Jewish people are referred to as "the children of Israel," a reference to the fact that they are all the physical or spiritual descendants of the patriarch Jacob, who was later named Israel. In other words, Jews are part of his extended family.

Major Types of Judaism Today

Orthodox: Believes the Torah (books of Moses) was written by God and is to be followed today. Ten percent of American Jews claim to be Orthodox.

Reform: Does not believe the Torah was written by Moses. Considered the liberals of Judaism, Reform Jews follow the principles of the Torah rather than specific commandments. Thirty-five percent of America's Jewish population is made up of Reform Jews.

Conservative: A middle ground between Orthodox and Reform Judaism, they believe the Torah came from God but contains human components as well. Twenty-six percent of American Jews consider themselves Conservatives.[7]

Messianic: Messianic Jews are Jewish Christians. Reports claim 280 congregations with over 47,000 followers worldwide.[8]

Judaism 101

What does Judaism believe and practice? The answer is more difficult to explain than you might think. Many Jewish leaders have suggested various lists of common beliefs, but the most accepted is the list of 13 principles of faith by Rabbi Rambam (A.D. 1135–1204):

1. God exists.
2. God is one and unique (Deuteronomy 6:4 says that the Lord is one).
3. God is incorporeal (invisible).
4. God is eternal.
5. Prayer is to be directed to God alone and to no other.

6. The words of the prophets are true.

7. Moses' prophecies are true, and Moses was the greatest of the prophets.

8. The Written Torah (first 5 books of the Bible) and Oral Torah (teachings now contained in the Talmud and other writings) were given to Moses.

9. There will be no other Torah.

10. God knows the thoughts and deeds of men.

11. God will reward the good and punish the wicked.

12. The Messiah will come.

13. The dead will be resurrected.[9]

Judaism tends to focus more on actions than beliefs. For example, the emphasis in Orthodox Judaism is the practice of the 613 commandments of the Torah and their interpretation in the later writings of the rabbis. Many of today's books on Judaism focus on Jewish practices regarding special days, holidays, and other traditions.

Despite the heavy emphasis on actions, it is important to note that Judaism consists of more than rules and regulations. The attitudes of their religion can best be explained through the word *halakhah,* a Hebrew verb meaning "to go, walk, or travel." The goal of observing Jewish law is to increase spirituality, not simply to increase obedience. Through the practice of Jewish law, a person grows closer to God and to other people, and this results in a more meaningful way of life.

Jewish Persecutions

Throughout their history, Jews have encountered much hatred and persecution, usually without provocation on their own part. Many people are aware of the tragedies that took place during the Holocaust during World War II, but there are many other instances of Jewish persecution in the past and today:

- Slavery in Egypt prior to the exodus led by Moses.
- Invasions and conquests by Assyrians and Babylonians

during Old Testament times (approximately 2500 years ago).

- The Crusades of the Middle Ages, during which more than 10,000 Jews were killed in Christian Europe.

- Anti-Semitism during the Spanish Inquisition and up through the early Protestant Reformation. Even the German reformer Martin Luther wrote of discriminating against Jews who rejected Christianity during his time.

- Current ongoing anti-Semitism from radical Muslims and neo-Nazis who seek the harm of Jewish people.

Judaism and Christianity

Christianity actually began as a sect within Judaism. Jesus and the first Christians were Jews and practiced many Jewish traditions alongside their Christian beliefs. However, after Jesus' death, resurrection, and ascension to heaven, Jewish religious leaders began to persecute Christians, removing them from local synagogues. This, along with the spread of Christianity among non-Jews throughout the Roman Empire of the first century, eventually resulted in Christianity being viewed as a separate religion.

Adapted from ReligionFacts.com, the chart on page 57 shows some of the major comparisons between Christianity and Judaism:

Comparison of Basic Concepts in Judaism and Christianity[10]

	Judaism	Christianity
adherents called	Jews	Christians
current adherents	14 million	2 billion
sacred text	Bible	Bible (Jewish Bible + New Testament)
other written authority	Talmud, Midrash, Responsa	church fathers, church councils, papal decrees (Catholic only)
religious law	halakhah	canon law
clergy	rabbis	ministers, pastors, bishops (priests in Roman Catholicism)
house of worship	synagogue	church, chapel, cathedral
main day of worship	Saturday	Sunday

The foundational belief difference in Christianity is that it accepts Jesus of Nazareth as the Son of God and the promised Jewish Messiah. After the death and resurrection of Jesus, some of his key followers recorded his teachings and wrote what resulted in the 27-book collection known as the New Testament. Of course, Jews believe these teachings represent false views that must be rejected and continue to wait for their promised Messiah. However, Christian scholarship has shown that as many as 456 of the Jewish prophecies regarding the identity of the Messiah fit Jesus and only Jesus.

Here are just eight specific prophecies regarding the Jewish Messiah that are true of Jesus:

- Genesis 12:1-3 predicts the Messiah would come from the family line of Abraham.
- Genesis 49:10 predicts the Messiah would come from the tribe of Judah.

- Second Samuel 7:12 predicts the Messiah would come from the ancestry of King David.

- Micah 5:2 predicts the Messiah would be born in the city of Bethlehem.

- Daniel 9:24-26 predicts the Messiah would die or be "cut off" exactly 483 years after the declaration to reconstruct the temple (this declaration was made in in 444 B.C.).

- Isaiah 53 predicts the Messiah would die with thieves, then be buried in the tomb of someone affluent.

- Psalm 22:16 predicts that his hands and feet would be pierced (which took place at the cross). This is quite significant because Roman crucifixion had not yet been invented at the time the psalmist wrote these words.

- Isaiah 49:7 predicts that the Messiah would be known and hated by the entire nation. Not many men become known by their entire nation, and even fewer are despised by an entire nation.

What is the possibility of someone fulfilling these prophecies by coincidence? Pat Zukeran writes:

> Let us suppose you estimate there is a one in a hundred chance a man could fulfill just one of these prophecies by chance. That would mean when all eight are put together there is a 1/10 to the 16th power probability that they were fulfilled by chance. Mathematician Peter Stoner estimates 1/10 to the seventeenth power possibility that these prophecies were fulfilled by chance. Mathematicians have estimated that the possibility of sixteen of these prophecies being fulfilled by chance are about 1/10 to the 45th power. That's a decimal point followed by 44 zeroes and a 1! These figures show it is extremely improbable that these prophecies could have been fulfilled by accident. The figures for fulfillment of the 109 major prophecies are staggering.[11]

We have looked at only eight prophecies, yet the Bible records *456 specific prophecies* concerning the Messiah.[12] Anyone who could fit the profile of hundreds of unique characteristics predicted hundreds of years earlier by multiple people would have to be given very serious consideration.

In summary, the basic similarities and differences between biblical Christianity and Judaism appear in the chart below:

Belief	Jewish Perspective	Biblical Perspective
God	There is only one God; no acknowledgment of the Trinity.	One God in three persons— Father, Son, and Holy Spirit.
Holy Book	The 39 books of the Old Testament are considered revelation from God, especially the Torah (first five books). The New Testament is rejected.	The 66 books of the Holy Bible are the authoritative works of Christianity.
Sin	All people have sinned. However, many Jews do not believe in the concept of original sin (humans are born with a sinful nature).	All people have sinned and every person is born with original sin (except Jesus).
Jesus Christ	Views vary, though all would claim that Jesus is not the Son of God or the Messiah sent by God. Some view him as a good teacher, others as a heretical teacher, and still others as a legend.	God's perfect son, holy, resurrected, divine (second person of the Trinity), yet also fully human, God's Messiah (Isaiah 52:13– 53:12) and the "son of Man" (Daniel 7:13-14).
Salvation	Judaism admits the existence of sin and the necessity for atonement, but has not developed a system of salvation teaching as found in Christianity. Atonement is accomplished by sacrifices, penitence, good deeds, and a little of God's grace.	Obtained only by God's grace through faith in Jesus Christ, not by human effort. "Now there have been many of those priests, since death prevented them from continuing in office; but because Jesus lives forever, he has a permanent

priesthood. Therefore he is able to save completely those who come to God through him, because he always lives to intercede for them" (Hebrews 7:23-25).

"Therefore let all Israel be assured of this: God has made this Jesus, whom you crucified, both Lord and Christ" (Acts 2:36).

| Afterlife | God will reward the good and punish the wicked. | At death, all people will enter heaven or hell based on whether they have salvation in Jesus Christ. The Bible does not support the view that God awards heaven to people who have done good deeds. A holy God requires a perfect sacrifice for our sins, a sacrifice that only Christ could provide. |

As we consider the big deal about Judaism, it is important to note that Christianity is built upon the historical backdrop of the Jewish Scriptures. In addition, the historical and cultural influence of Judaism has made a marked impact on our planet. However, to say that there are no major differences between Jewish beliefs and biblical Christianity would be a completely inaccurate statement.

Both religions believe in a Messiah, but Christians believe he has already come while Jews are still waiting for his arrival. In the end, the big deal is that Judaism and Christianity have a familiar foundation, but differ on who Jesus is—whether he is the Messiah, the Son of God, the one who will judge the world at the end of time (Matthew 25:31-33). Again, one or the other can be right, but they can't both be right at the same time.

When we examine the beliefs of Judaism, we find that it differs from biblical Christianity in all six of our major belief categories. Since all six areas are foundational in Christianity, we can see that Judaism's distinctions are a big deal to Christianity. The goal of Christians is to present the evidence for Christ's claims, point out the predictions spelled out by the Jewish prophets in the Old Testament, and show genuine love for those who follow Judaism. Their desire is to actively share and live out their beliefs to those of Jewish faith in order to communicate the big deal about Jesus for the lives of Jews today.

Is Allah Really
4 | **the Only God?**

n only 1400 years since its inception, Islam has become the second largest religion in the world, with over one billion adherents.[1] It is growing by about 68,000 people every 24 hours, and expanding rapidly in the United States. In Dearborn, Michigan, for example, 40,000 of the 100,000 residents are of Muslim background.[2] Yet while Islam has become more widespread in recent years, many non-Muslims have little knowledge of its beginnings, beliefs, or practices.

Since the tragedy of 9/11, American interest in Islamic beliefs has grown greatly. In 2006, I (John) had the opportunity to interview two brothers who had converted from Islam to Christianity and now serve as professors in major Christian universities. Speaking of the differences between Christianity and the other one-God religions, one of these men, Dr. Ergun Caner, president of Liberty Seminary, noted,

> You can summarize the difference between Christianity and Islam in the Islamic mind by saying: the Jew had the truth, lost it, and corrupted it. Then the Christian had the truth, lost it, and corrupted it. Then comes Muhammad, the final hope. So he saves us, he protects, and receives from the Angel Gabriel the absolute truth, which is Islam.

Christianity, Judaism, and all other world systems are seen as ghosts, empty shells of themselves. This was our view. This was what we thought of anything that was Christian.[3]

Because Islam believes it is the one true religion and that all other religions are corrupted, anyone who wants to communicate effectively with Muslims must gain a clear understanding of Islam's origins and worldview. Together, let's look at how Islam began, its five pillars, its holy book the Qur'an, and its major beliefs.

Muslim Origins

The early history of Islam revolved around one central figure, Muhammad. Muhammad was born around A.D. 570 in the city of Mecca in Arabia. His father died before his birth. His mother died when he was six. He was raised first by his grandfather and later by his uncle. Muhammad's early background is not well known. Some scholars believe he came from a well-respected family, but this is uncertain.

At the age of 25, Muhammad married a wealthy 40-year-old widow named Khadijah. During this time, Muhammad came to believe in only one God, Allah, and rejected the idolatrous polytheism of those around him. By the age of 40, the now-religious Muhammad had his first vision. These revelations were later said to be recorded in the Qur'an.

At first Muhammad was unsure if his visions were from God or demonic spirits. His wife, Khadijah, encouraged him to believe that they had come from God. Later she became his first convert. Muhammad's most important early convert was a wealthy merchant named Abu Bakr, who eventually became one of his successors. *The Cambridge History of Islam* comments on Muhammad's revelations:

> Either in the course of the visions or shortly afterwards, Muhammad began to receive "messages" or "revelations" from God. Sometimes he may have heard the words being spoken to him, but for the most part he seems simply to

have "found them in his heart." Whatever the precise "manner of revelation"—and several different "manners" were listed by Muslim scholars—the important point is that the message was not the product of Muhammad's conscious mind. He believed that he could easily distinguish between his own thinking and these revelations.

The messages, which thus came to Muhammad from beyond his conscious mind were at first fairly short, and consisted of short verses ending in a common rhyme or assonance. They were committed to memory by Muhammad and his followers, and recited as part of their common worship. Muhammad continued to receive the messages at intervals until his death. In his closing years the revelations tended to be longer, to have much longer verses and to deal with the affairs of the community of Muslims at Medina. All, or at least many, of the revelations were probably written down during Muhammad's lifetime by his secretaries.[4]

Muhammad's first visions marked the start of his prophetic call by Allah. Muhammad received these visions for the next 22 years until his death in A.D. 632.

Muhammad's new faith encountered opposition in his own hometown of Mecca. Because of this rejection, Muhammad and his followers withdrew to the city known as Medina. The *hijira,* which means "flight," marked the turning point in Islam. All Islamic calendars mark this date, July 16, 622, as their beginning. So, for example, A.D. 630 corresponds to 8 A.H. (in the year of the hijira).

In Muhammad's early years in Medina, when he had few followers, he was sympathetic to both Jews and Christians, but they rejected him and his teaching. Upon that rejection, Muhammad turned from Jerusalem as the center of worship of Islam to Mecca, where the famous black stone Ka'aba is located. Muhammad denounced all the idols that surrounded the Ka'aba and declared it was a shrine for the one true God, Allah.

With this new emphasis on Mecca, Muhammad realized he must soon return to his home. The rejected prophet made a return, in triumph, conquering the city by force. Muhammad next secured his political and prophetic leadership in Arabia. Active opponents were killed or conquered through warfare. Tribes far away from Mecca were invited to send delegations offering their allegiance to Muhammad. Before his sudden death in 632, he knew he was well on the way to unifying the Arab tribes under a theocracy governed by the will of Allah. In the years before his death, Muhammad zealously and militantly propagated Islam, and the new faith quickly spread throughout Arabia.[5]

After Muhammad's death, a power struggle developed regarding a successor. The major division came between those who believed the caliph (leader) should be elected by the Islamic leadership (today known as Sunnis) and those who believed the successor should be hereditary, through 'Ali, Muhammad's son-in-law, who was married to his only daughter, Fatima (today known as Shiites). Sunnis, Shiites, and Sufis are the three major branches of Islam today.

The Difference Between Judaism and Islam

"The real difference between the two religions...lies in their basis for belief. Judaism is based on the unique historical event of a divine revelation experienced by the entire nation [Moses and the Exodus from Egypt and the sojourn through the desert to the land of Israel], whereas Islam is based on the prophetic claims of a single individual who subsequently convinced others to follow his ways."[6]

The Five Pillars

Muslims follow the teachings of the Qur'an (where every word is Allah's) and Hadith (an authoritative collection of Muhammad's sayings and practices). Foremost of their practices are the five pillars of Islam. These include:

> 1. *To recite* the shahadah: This is the reciting of the creed, "There is no God but Allah, and Muhammad is His messenger."

2. *To pray* (salat): This includes 17 prayers per day, prayer at noon at a mosque on Fridays, and five specified times of prayer daily.

3. *To fast* (sawm): During the lunar month of Ramadhan, Muslims refrain from food during the daylight hours and only eat at night.

4. *To give alms* (zakat): Muslims are required to give one-fortieth of their income (2.5 percent) to the poor and needy.

5. *To make the pilgrimage* (hajj): Those physically and financially able must visit Mecca at least once during their lifetime. The journey usually takes at least a week, including many stops at other holy sites along the way.[7]

The Sixth Pillar?

Jihad is a sixth religious duty often associated with the five pillars of Islam, although it is considered by many analysts and scholars in modern times to be optional. But in Arab Muslim culture, the consensus on the meaning of jihad is much narrower, and definitely draws from historical accounts and religious citations from the Qur'an and Hadith. Jihad may be interpreted as internal (the spiritual struggle to prepare for the external) or external (defending or advancing Islam when called upon to do so). When Muslim leaders believe the situation warrants it, this duty requires Muslims to go to war to defend Islam against its enemies, or to advance the borders of the House of Islam in order to protect and secure its borders. Anyone who dies in a holy war is allegedly guaranteed eternal life in heaven and is considered a martyr for Islam.[8]

In his groundbreaking and controversial book *Future Jihad*, Walid Phares notes the historical usage of jihad, "The inner cleansing...was to better prepare for the [external] jihad in the public sphere. At least until secular modernity developed in many areas of the Muslim world, the real, greater jihad was a state doctrine."[9] Historically, jihad (war) has been used in Islam as the theological basis for advancing the house of Islam, securing its borders by advancing its borders, reacquiring lands once in the house of Islam (such as Israel), or defensively in war against other nations, a pattern that some Muslims continue to observe in the Islamic world today.

Dr. Emir Caner, dean of the college at Southwestern Baptist Theological Seminary in Fort Worth, Texas, explains the implications of Islam's pillars:

> The pillars of Islam really demonstrate that Islam is *a works-based religion*. Not only reciting the creed, 'There is no God but Allah, and Muhammad is his prophet,' and saying it tens of thousands of times through your life; but the prayers five times daily; the fasting which is one lunar month out of the year; and going to Mecca; and doing the tithe. These five pillars encompass your entire life.[10]

The idea in Islam is that if you perform well enough in these five areas, you have a better chance to obtain a joyful afterlife. This obedience to a set of regulations sets Islam apart from Christianity, which says salvation and heaven come only through belief in Jesus Christ.

Qur'an 101

The Qur'an has been called the world's most memorized book, and rightly so. A requirement of all Muslims is to memorize its contents. Its 114 chapters (called *Suras*) are believed to include Allah's word-for-word final revelation to his people. Therefore, if anything in the Qur'an contradicts "earlier revelation" found in other holy books (such as the Bible), the Qur'an's teachings supersede those books and alone is correct.

Interestingly, the Qur'an includes many individuals and stories already mentioned in the Jewish and Christian Scriptures. Abraham, Moses, Jesus, and many other Bible personalities are noted in positive ways. Some of the Qur'an's key stories also closely resemble stories found in the Bible.

Other Holy Writings in Islam

The Hadith: These are collections of Muhammad's sayings and practices that are not included in the Qur'an. Hadiths have been collected and communicated by various Islamic scholars.

The Qiyas: These include communal agreements by Muslims regarding interpretations of the Qur'an and Hadith.

The Shari'ah: A collection of laws for Muslims to follow, similar to civil laws in Western cultures. Many Islamic countries are currently governed by what is called shari'ah law.

Upon a closer reading, however, we find that Islam teaches that both the Torah (books of Moses) and the Injil (the Gospels) were corrupted or misinterpreted by Jews and Christians. On the other hand, the Qur'an alone remains perfect and pure in Muslim eyes.

How was the Qur'an compiled? According to tradition, Allah gave his prophet Muhammad several revelations through the angel Gabriel. Muhammad dictated these revelations to his followers, who wrote them down (*Qur'an* means "the reciting" or "the reading"). After Muhammad's death, Abu Bakr commissioned Zaid ibn Thabit to track down the existing portions of the Qur'an to create one unified book. Though other lists of portions were later collected, Muslim leaders decided that Zaid's list would become the standard for the Islamic movement. Today, Muslims claim the present Qur'an is an exact copy of Muhammad's original revelations (in spite of the fact other portions of the Qur'an exist that were not included in the current volume).

The Qur'an and the Bible

Unlike the texts of the Bible, written by a number of authors over an extended period of time, the Qur'an claims to be the work of one man. Though both Islam and Christianity believe their sacred texts are inspired works, Muslims don't typically attempt to "prove" the accuracy or inspiration of the Qur'an because they are satisfied to say that it came directly from Allah. Christians, however, usually offer historical research that affirms the reliability of Scripture and their claim that the Bible is God's true inspired Word.

Basic Beliefs

There are five basic Muslim beliefs that are foundational to all the others:[11]

There is only one God and Allah is his name.

According to Dr. Jamal Badawi, chairman of the Islamic Information Foundation, Muslims believe that:

> God is one in essence and in person. This excludes the presence of equal divine persons in the same Godhead. Neither tritheism nor Trinity, however explained, is compatible with pure Islamic monotheism. Two, God alone is worthy of worship and unqualified devotion. None is to be worshipped instead of Him or alongside Him as co-equal, nor is God to be worshipped through any creature whether religious institution, clergy, or even the greatest of the prophets. The third condition in Islam for monotheism is that any shortcoming, man-like weakness, or limitation is not befitting to the glory of God. This excludes any notion of God incarnate and any other quality or action which is ungod-like or unsuitable for the majesty of God.
>
> To the Muslim, any deviation from any of these conditions means to associate or join others with God in His exclusive, divine attributes. It is regarded as a serious compromise of pure and longstanding monotheism taught by all prophets. In fact, Muslims believe that prophet Muhammad, peace be upon him, was sent by God to restore and clarify the same pure concept of monotheism that was taught by all the prophets.[12]

But if God wanted to, would it be possible for him to inhabit a human body and, at the same time, keep all his attributes? Christianity teaches that Jesus is the God-man, fully God and fully human in one person.

There have been many prophets, including Noah,
Abraham, Moses, Jesus, and Muhammad.

As in Judaism and Christianity, Islam accepts the idea of prophets who can predict future events. The Qur'an names over 20 prophets, including Adam, Noah, Abraham, Moses, David, Jonah, and John the Baptist. In total, Muslims believe Allah has sent over 100,000 prophets throughout history.

Jesus is also listed as a prophet in the Qur'an. Though the Qur'an accepts that Jesus lived a sinless life, Muslims do not believe he was God's son. In fact, to believe that Jesus is divine is considered blasphemy.

Do Muslims Believe Jesus Is God's Son?

In contrast with Christianity, Islam believes that Jesus was only *one* of God's endless prophets or messengers. The Qur'an repeatedly emphasizes that Jesus Christ is not the literal son of God:

- "They say, 'God has taken to Him a son'...Say: 'Those who forge against God falsehood shall not prosper.'"[13]

- "Praise belongs to God [Allah], who has not taken to Him a son...."[14]

- "Warn those who say, 'God has taken to Himself a son'...a monstrous word it is, issuing out of their mouths; they say nothing but a lie."[15]

- "But who does greater evil than he who forges against God a lie?"[16]

- "They are unbelievers who say, 'God is the Messiah, Mary's Son.'"[17]

The Qur'an emphatically denies that Jesus Christ is the son of God, whereas Jesus himself said the opposite (John 3:16,18; 10:36-38).[18] The following chart highlights these differences:

Comparing Jesus in Islam and Christianity

Muslim Jesus	Sura	Biblical Jesus	Verses
Jesus was created	3:59	Jesus is eternal	Micah 5:2
Jesus was human	3:59	Jesus is human and divine	John 1:1,14
Jesus was not crucified	4:157	Jesus died on the cross for our sins	John 1:29; 19:17-18
The five pillars provide salvation	9:20-22; 4:124	Jesus provides salvation	Acts 4:12

Jesus did not die, therefore he did not rise from the dead	4:157	Jesus rose from the dead	John 11:25; 20:10-18
Jesus is not to be worshipped	5:75	Jesus is to be worshipped	Philippians 2:10-11
Jesus was just another prophet	2:136; 2:84	Jesus is the name above all names	Ephesians 1:21; Philippians 2:9

Islam claims that Jesus was merely a prophet. But was he more than a prophet? Why was Jesus convicted and sentenced to death by the Jewish Sanhedrin? Because when he was asked, "Are you the Son of God?" he said that he was (see Mark 14:61-64).

God created angels (jinn), some of which are good and others evil.

The Qur'an teaches the existence of both good and bad angels who are invisible beings and live at a level between humans and Allah. Various ranks of angels exist, and there are four primary archangels (Jibrail, the Angel of Death, Mikail, Israphil).

Each human being is believed to have two angels who record all the good and evil acts a person commits during his or her lifetime. These angels later play an important role in the person's life on judgment day.

In biblical Christianity, angels are messengers of God who serve God and assist people as God sees fit. On judgment day, Jesus Christ will be the judge of all the nations and every person who has ever lived (Matthew 7:21-23; John 5:25-27).

The Qur'an is God's full and final revelation.

The Qur'an is Islam's most sacred text and serves as God's final and perfect revelation to Muslims. The Qur'an is considered desecrated if a person defiles or dismembers it. Muslims treat the book with great reverence and are forbidden to recycle or simply discard worn-out copies. Respect for the written text of the Qur'an is an important element of the Islamic faith. They believe that intentionally insulting the Qur'an is a form of blasphemy. According to the laws of some Muslim countries, such blasphemy is punishable by lengthy imprisonment or even the death penalty.[19]

By contrast, biblical Christianity believes the 66 books of the Bible are God's revelation to humanity as affirmed by Jesus (Matthew 4:4; Luke 24:27) and the apostles (2 Timothy 3:15-17; 2 Peter 1:19-21).

A final day of judgment is coming, followed by heaven for the faithful and hell for the lost.

Islam teaches that on the day of judgment one's good and evil deeds will be weighed on a scale. Those whose balances are heavy with good deeds will go to heaven, while those whose scales are light in regard to good deeds will go to hell. The Qur'an teaches:

- "[In the day of judgment] they whose balances shall be heavy with good works, shall be happy; but they whose balances shall be light, are those who shall lose their souls, and shall remain in hell forever."[20]

- "With knowledge We will recount to them what they have done, for We are watching over all their actions. On that day [of judgment], their deeds shall be weighed with justice. Those whose scales are heavy [with good works] shall triumph, but those whose scales are light shall lose their souls, because they have denied Our revelations [e.g., in the Qur'an]."[21]

The Muslim assumes that his chances for heaven are good if he accepts the Muslim God Allah and his prophet Muhammad, does good works and all that is required of him by Allah, and is predestined to Allah's favor.

Given such requirements, can Muslims have any assurance of salvation? Abdiyah Akbar Abdul-Haqq comments that the Islamic reliance on good works is bound to leave any Muslim who seeks for personal assurance of salvation completely confused.[22] No Muslim can ever know if his good works are sufficient or if he has been predestined to Allah's favor or damnation.[23]

Jesus, however, taught that all people are sinners with no possibility of being good enough to earn their way to heaven. God loves all sinful men and women and has provided salvation as a gift by having his righteous son die as an atoning sacrifice for every person's sins. Because Christ did all that God requires, once we admit we are sinners and place our total trust in what Christ did for us, we are given the gift of salvation, which includes eternal life (John 3:16; 8:24).

Major Divisions of Islam

Sunni: Sunni Islam is the largest branch of Islam. According to some sources, approximately 85 percent of the world's Muslims are Sunni. Unlike in Shi'as, Sunnis believe that Muhammad died without appointing a successor to lead the Muslim community. Any good Muslim leader can lead.

Shi'a: Shi'a Islam is the second largest division of Islam. Shi'a Muslims believe that Ali was appointed by Muhammad to be the direct successor and leader of the Muslim community. They regard him as the first Imam, which then continued as a hereditary position through Ali's descendants. Approximately 15 percent of Muslims are Shi'a.

Sufi: An umbrella term for the mystical movements within Islam, Sufism is the school of esoteric (secret) Islamic philosophy and is based on the pursuit of spiritual truth as a definite goal to attain. The primary trait all Sufis share in common is a mystical, esoteric view of faith and God.[24]

The Big Deal About Islam

The big deal about Islam is well summarized from the writings of our friends Dr. Ergun Caner and Dr. Emir Caner. Together, they write:

> Islam teaches that Allah's love and forgiveness is conditioned upon one's righteousness (Surah 2:279; 17:25; 19:60). The Bible teaches that God's love and forgiveness is unconditional, based not on how good one has been, but on the death of Jesus. Jesus paid the infinite cost of sin on behalf of those who accept that atonement for their own

lives (Romans 10:9-10,13). Salvation is not founded upon the enduring work of each person but on the finished work of Christ (John 19:30). To maintain that Jesus Christ died for the world affects one's theology. To admit that Jesus Christ died for me affects my eternal destiny.[25]

In other words, Islam is a big deal to Christians because it denies that Jesus is God's son, teaches that heaven is obtained through human effort rather than God's grace, and teaches that the Bible is a corrupted book. These and other foundational differences show that these two faiths are vastly different. Those who claim to follow Jesus find in Muslims a deeply spiritual people who have a completely different understanding of the basic beliefs Christians hold to be of great importance.

As we view Islam at a glance, we find the following clear distinctions:

Belief	Muslim Perspective	Biblical Perspective
God	There is only one God named Allah. No acknowledgment of the Trinity.	One God in three persons— Father, Son, and Holy Spirit.
	Sura 5:73 in the Qur'an: "They do blaspheme who say God is one of three...for there is no Allah except one Allah."	
Holy Book	The Qur'an is Islam's holy book. Parts of the Hadith and other holy writings are also studied as religious literature. The Bible is considered a good book, but corrupted.	The 66 books of the Bible are the authoritative works of Christianity and reveal God's truth to humanity.
Sin	All people have sinned. However, Islam does not believe in original sin (that humans are born with a sinful nature).	All people have sinned (except Jesus).

Jesus Christ	A good man but not God. Those who believe Jesus is God are considered unbelievers.	God's perfect son, holy, resurrected, divine (second person of the Trinity), yet also fully human.
Salvation	Completely based on human effort, especially the practice of the five pillars. Sura 11:114: "For those things that are good remove those that are evil." One exception is that those who die as martyrs in war will receive eternal paradise (Sura 3:157).	Obtained only by God's grace through faith in Jesus Christ, not by human effort.
Afterlife	The person whose balances are heavy with good deeds will go to heaven (called paradise), while the person whose scales are light will go to hell. Heaven is described in much different terms in the Qur'an than in the Bible.	At death, all people will enter either heaven or hell based on whether they have salvation in Jesus Christ.

Though Islam is the only other major world religion to believe in one God outside of Judaism and Christianity, it holds to completely different beliefs from Christianity in every major area. In fact, even the "one God" that Islam believes in is distinctly different in name and definition than the God of Christianity. To suggest that these two religions are basically the same or follow the same God is not accurate.

Islam and biblical Christianity may share some similar traits, but they hold to several foundational and irreconcilable differences. They are not two ways to the same God, but rather two religious systems with radically different beliefs and two different Gods. According to biblical Christianity, those who follow Muslim teachings are following a false God, false teachings, and need a relationship with the true God through Jesus Christ in order to spend eternity in heaven.

If you are a Muslim reading this chapter, take a moment to think about these questions: Do God's prophets tell the truth? Yes, they do. Then why did the Jewish leaders conclude Jesus was guilty of death? Was it because they asked him this specific question: "Are you the Christ, the Son of the Blessed One [the son of God]?"

History records that Jesus answered by stating, "I am" (Mark 14:61-62). On this basis the Jewish religious leaders condemned him to death. Our question to you is this: Did the prophet Jesus lie or tell the truth? If he told the truth, then wouldn't you agree that Jesus, according to his own words, must be much more than a prophet? If Jesus was telling the truth, then he is truly the son of God. If you are interested in investigating this issue more, we encourage you to please see the last chapter of this book and learn about how to begin a relationship with God through Jesus and to consider reading some additional resources about Jesus, which we've listed in that chapter.

Part Three: | Popular
Alternative
Religions

n addition to the big three "one God" religions of Christianity, Judaism, and Islam, several alternative religions have become popular in North America today. Because we are not attempting to discuss every religious movement in the United States, we have chosen to focus on four of the most significant and influential alternative religions today.

First, we'll take a look at Mormonism. Though some view Mormonism as a group within Christianity, we'll observe that its history and beliefs do not match up with those of biblical Christianity. I (John) have invited Mormon leaders on our television program and interviewed them regarding what they believe, and it's clear they stand apart from Christianity. I have also interviewed the great-great-great granddaughter of Brigham Young (the second prophet of the Mormon Church), who, as a college student, was challenged as to the truthfulness of her Mormon beliefs. She examined the evidence and left the Mormon Church to become a true biblical Christian. We will talk about the differences between Mormonism and Christianity in the upcoming chapter.

Next we'll investigate the history and religious practices of the Jehovah's Witnesses, one of the fastest-spreading new religious movements founded in the United States. With more than 6.5 million followers worldwide, this group has established itself as a major force.

Third, we'll take a look into the world of Kabbalah, a mystical form of Judaism whose recent popularity has attracted some of Hollywood's elite. Though tied to one of the world's oldest religions, we'll find that its development is more recent than often suggested and its ideas are much more different from those of Orthodox Judaism than often claimed.

Finally, our journey will lead us into an investigation of Wicca, claimed by some experts to be the fastest-spreading religion in America today. Now officially a religion according the U.S. Armed Forces and accepted as the basis for legal marriages in the United Kingdom, Wicca's influence has reached far beyond mere media mentions and into the mainstream of Western culture.

Aren't Mormons
5 Christians?

ccording to the Church of Jesus Christ of Latter-day Saints...

- there are more than 12 million members in the Mormon Church

- over 50,000 Mormon missionaries work in over 200 countries worldwide

- more than 4.6 million copies of the Book of Mormon are distributed each year

- The Book of Mormon has been translated into 105 different languages

- Mormons baptize approximately 300,000 new converts each year [1]

Mormonism, or the Church of Jesus Christ of Latter-day Saints, is one of the largest and fastest-growing religious movements in existence today. In less than 200 years, the Mormon movement has touched over 200 nations and developed a missionary force that rivals those of the largest religious groups in the world.

On a more personal level, Mormons are also probably some of the friendliest people we run into. They emphasize family values, good morals, and community involvement. Following high school, every Mormon is required to serve for two years as a missionary. A required ten-percent tithe from all church members means financial support that could go as high as 30 billion dollars per year. In many ways, statistics show the Mormon movement to be extremely impressive.

But what do Mormons believe? Ask someone who is Mormon, and he or she will probably claim to be a Christian. Mormons say they believe in Jesus and the Christian Bible. Their moral lives may even look better than that of many Christians.

While a surface examination reveals several similarities, our conversation changes when we look under the hood of Mormonism and examine its history and beliefs. In almost every area of faith, Mormonism contrasts or contradicts traditional Christianity. Our journey together in this chapter will include a look at Mormon history, its sacred writings, its beliefs, and some ideas for Christians who desire to talk to those who follow the Mormon faith.

Mormon Influence

"With unusual cooperation from the Latter-day Saints hierarchy (which provided some financial figures and a rare look at church businesses), *Time* has been able to quantify the church's extra-ordinary financial vibrancy. Its current assets total a minimum of $30 billion. If it were a corporation, its estimated $5.9 billion in annual gross income would place it midway through the Fortune 500, a little below Union Carbide and the Paine Webber Group but bigger than Nike and the Gap."[2]

—*TIME* MAGAZINE

A Historical Tour of Mormonism

The Mormon Church was founded by Joseph Smith. Born in 1805 in Vermont, he grew up in upstate New York. According to his recollections, he had a vision in 1820 at the age of 15 in which he saw and heard the following:

> It was on the morning of a beautiful clear day, early in the spring of eighteen hundred and twenty...I saw a pillar of light exactly over my head...When the light rested upon

me I saw two personages (whose brightness and glory defy all description) standing above me in the air. One of them spoke unto me, calling me by name, and said (pointing to the other), "This is my beloved Son, hear him"...I asked the personages who stood above me in the light, which of all the sects was right...I was answered that I must join none of them, for they were all wrong, and the personage who addressed me said that all their creeds were an abomination in his sight...[3]

In other words, all the existing Christian denominations of Joseph Smith's day were wrong and their creeds were an abomination. Joseph was not to join any of them. Rather, he was to start his own church. He believed he had been directly commanded by God the Father and Jesus, whom he states were the "two personages."

Three years later, Joseph Smith said he had another vision. This time, the angel Moroni appeared to him and told him that near his home there was a book written upon gold plates that included information about the former inhabitants of America, the true gospel, and accounts from the "Savior."

After another three years, young Joseph, then 21, discovered these hidden writings and began to translate them into English from "Egyptian hieroglyphics." This translation became known as the Book of Mormon and was published in 1830, beginning Joseph's movement as he preached and gained converts in the Midwest.

The center of Joseph Smith's movement began in the small town of Nauvoo, Illinois, of which he became mayor and leader of the local army. During this time, Joseph claimed to continue receiving numerous revelations on a myriad of spiritual topics.

By April of 1844, when Joseph Smith preached at the funeral of Elder King Follet, his theology had emerged. A portion of that message, heard by more than 18,000 people and recorded by four Mormon scribes, stated:

I want you all to know God, to be familiar with him... What sort of a being was God in the beginning? First, God himself, who sits enthroned in yonder heavens, is a man like unto one of yourselves...I am going to tell you how God came to be God...to know for a certainty the character of God, that we may converse with him as one man with another, and that God himself, the Father of us all dwelt on an earth the same as Jesus Christ himself did...Here then is eternal life, to know the only wise and true God. You have got to learn how to be Gods yourselves...by going from a small degree to another, from grace to grace, from exaltation to exaltation, until you are to sit in glory as do those who sit enthroned in everlasting power.[4]

Though many of Smith's beliefs and practices were controversial, the matter that stirred the most vocal opposition was Joseph's personal practice of polygamy. He had more than 30 wives, which led many to begin questioning his religious leadership. He was arrested and imprisoned in Nauvoo, where an angry mob stormed the jail and killed him.

Brigham Young, one of the leaders in the early Mormon movement, assumed leadership of the church after Joseph Smith's death. In 1847, Young led the faithful to Utah, where they established Salt Lake City. The city continued to serve as a religious capital until 1890, at which time it became the capital of the new state of Utah. However, the city continues to serve as the spiritual nerve center of the movement today.

Mormon Scriptures

According to the Latter-day Saints *Gospel Principles* guide, the Mormon holy writings include the following:

What Scriptures Do We Have Today—The Church of Jesus Christ of Latter-day Saints accepts four books as scripture: the Bible, the Book of Mormon, the Doctrine and Covenants, and the Pearl of Great Price. These books are called the standard works of the Church. The inspired words of our [current] living prophets are also accepted as scripture.[5]

Let's look at these four standard Mormon works.

The Book of Mormon

The Book of Mormon contains Joseph Smith's translation of the materials he claimed were revealed to him by the angel Moroni. While Smith contended this was an inspired work, there are several key concerns many have raised upon evaluating it. First, where are the original gold plates used for Smith's translation work? Second, how could Smith, without specialized training, flawlessly translate large portions of unknown Egyptian hieroglyphics? How did the gold plates inscribed with Egyptian hieroglyphics arrive in the United States in the first place? Also, H. Michael Marquardt has noted that the Book of Mormon can easily be shown as a work of plagiarism of the King James Bible:

> Marquardt shows that the portion of the Book of Mormon that was supposed to have been written during the Old Testament period is literally peppered with phrases and quotations from the King James New Testament (he lists 200 examples). Even the "prophecies" appearing in the Old Testament portion of the book are often given in the New Testament wording that accompanies their fulfillment.[6]

In spite of these troubling problems, for those who follow Mormonism, the Book of Mormon stands as a sacred work and is used in all the movement's missionary efforts.

Doctrine and Covenants

Three years after Smith published the Book of Mormon, he authored the Book of Commandments. Two years later, he revised this work and retitled it Doctrine and Covenants. The current edition contains 138 sections and two official declarations. The first 135 sections contain Joseph Smith's revelations from 1823 to 1844, section 136 is a revelation from President Brigham Young in 1847, section 137 addresses the issues of salvation for the dead and for children, and section 138 documents a vision received by President Joseph

F. Smith in 1918. Declaration 1 is dated 1890 and is referred to as "The Manifesto." It contained new revelation declaring an end to the practice of polygamy. Declaration 2 is dated 1978 and declared that "all worthy male members" could now hold the priesthood and participate in the temple ceremonies. This ended the Mormon Church ban against African Americans becoming members.[7]

Pearl of Great Price

Pearl of Great Price contains the following:

- The Book of Moses—"An extract from the translation of the Bible as revealed to Joseph Smith the Prophet, June 1830–February 1831."

- The Book of Abraham—"A Translation of some ancient records, that have fallen into our hands from the catacombs of Egypt."

- Joseph Smith—Matthew—"An extract from the translation of the Bible as revealed to Joseph Smith the Prophet in 1831: Matthew 23:39 and chapter 24."

- Joseph Smith—History—"Extracts from the History of Joseph Smith, the Prophet. History of the Church, Vol.1, Chapters 1-5."

- The Articles of Faith. A list of 13 specific beliefs of the Mormon Church, written in 1842.

Prophecies Gone Awry in Mormon Writings

- Joseph Smith said that tall men dressed like Quakers live on the moon.
- Brigham Young said that men live on the sun.
- Joseph Smith prophesied that Jesus would return by 1891.
- Brigham Young prophesied that the Civil War would not free the slaves.[8]

The Mormon Bible

Joseph Smith believed the Bible translations of his time were corrupt and decided to create his own translation. This would have been extremely difficult to do because Smith did not know ancient Hebrew, Aramaic, or Greek (the Bible's original languages). What many non-Mormons have shown today is that Smith made thousands of changes to the popular King James Version of the Bible from his time. Interestingly, these changes included a prophecy in Genesis 50 that predicts the coming of Joseph Smith.

The Joseph Smith Translation of the Bible, also called the Inspired Version of the Bible or the JST, is a version of the Bible dictated by Joseph Smith. According to scholars, 3,410 Bible verses were in some way altered from the King James Version.[9]

Mormonism 101

While today's Mormons often claim they are Christians, a look at their foundational beliefs shows they are not. The following five areas of faith reveal some of the major areas of conflict:[10]

Ultimate Reality

- Matter and intelligence, the basic elements of all the worlds, are eternal [not God].
- There is an infinite number of gods producing other potential gods. No divine first cause exists.

God

- The God of Planet Earth (*Elohim*), our heavenly Father, is an exalted man who has a tangible human body. He came to be God through what is called "eternal pro- gression."
- God our heavenly Father is married to a multitude of wives, one of which is Jesus' heavenly Mother.
- There are many gods in other planets and in other universes.

- The Trinity consists of three separate gods.
- The Holy Ghost is distinct from the Holy Spirit.
- The potential exists for every man to become a god and every woman to become a goddess.

Creation

- The gods counseled together and created the present world order out of pre-existent matter.

Jesus Christ

- In heaven, Jesus was the firstborn spirit child of the heavenly Father and a heavenly mother. He is our elder brother. Jesus is also the brother of Lucifer, who became the devil.
- On earth, the Mormon Jesus was the product of a sexual relationship between God and Mary.
- Conceivably, Jesus was married and had children.

Mr. and Mrs. Jesus?

The Da Vinci Code wasn't the first major book to suggest Jesus was married. According to Mormon writings, Jesus was married "both to Mary and to Martha, whereby he could see his seed [children] before he was crucified."[11]

- Jesus' death on the cross made it possible for all men of every age to be resurrected. However, it was not sufficient to pay the price for all sin.
- Jesus was resurrected physically from the dead. He ascended visibly into heaven and will return visibly to earth one day.

Salvation

- In Mormonism, salvation includes the following: faith

in Jesus Christ, repentance, baptism, the laying on of hands, membership, keeping the commandments, accepting Joseph Smith and other church leaders as of God, and work within the temple.

- Upon death, Mormon salvation provides admittance, through resurrection, into one of three kingdoms, the Telestial kingdom, the Terrestrial kingdom (which includes those who were "honorable" people, but who did not accept the Mormon gospel in this life), and the Celestial kingdom. The highest of the three kingdoms is reserved for Mormons in good standing. There are three levels in this kingdom and only those who have been completely obedient to Mormon teaching, including marriage in a Mormon temple, may have a part in the highest heaven. They will enter it in family units and become gods.

Why Do Mormons Research Their Ancestors?

Mormon teachings state that "saving ordinances" must be made available to every individual who has ever lived. To make these ordinances available to people who did not have the opportunity to become Mormons while alive on earth, Mormons identify their ancestors and arrange for baptism and other ordinances to be performed for them by proxy—with a living person standing in for the deceased person—in a temple. Often referred to as temple work, this search for ancestors is an important element of the Mormon faith.[12]

Here is a comparison of Mormonism and biblical Christianity on the major elements of belief:

Belief	Mormon Perspective	Biblical Perspective
God	Many gods exist. The god of Earth has a tangible human body.	One God in three persons—Father, Son, and Holy Spirit.

Holy Book	Four holy books—The Mormon Bible, the Book of Mormon, Doctrine and Covenants, and Pearl of Great Price. Ongoing revelation is also given through prophets.	Only the 66 books of the Bible are the authoritative works of Christianity. The Bible also clearly teaches against adding to or changing the Scriptures, as done in the Mormon Bible (Revelation 22:18-19).
Sin	All people commit acts of sin. Original sin is denied (Mormons distinguish between "sin" and Adam's "transgression.").	All people have sinned and are born with a sin nature (except Jesus).
Jesus Christ	Jesus was the firstborn spirit child of the heavenly Father and a heavenly mother. He is our elder brother. Jesus is also the brother of Lucifer, who became the devil.	God's perfect son, holy, resurrected, divine (second person of the Trinity), yet also fully human.
Salvation	Salvation includes faith plus several specific works that must be done within the Mormon Church.	Obtained only by God's grace through faith in Jesus Christ, not by human effort.
Afterlife	All people enter one of three kingdoms: the Telestial kingdom, the Terrestrial kingdom, or the Celestial kingdom. People can become gods or goddesses.	At death, all people will enter heaven or hell based on whether they have salvation in Jesus Christ.

If Mormonism and biblical Christianity differ significantly in all six of the foundational beliefs upon which Christianity is built, what can we safely conclude? First, in answer to the question in the title of this chapter, Mormons are not Christians. Why? Mormonism believes in multiple gods, different holy books, a different Jesus, and different views of sin, salvation, and the afterlife.

The apostle Paul wrote, "If we or an angel from heaven should preach a gospel other than the one we preached to you, let him be eternally condemned! As we have already said, so now I say again: If anybody is preaching to you a gospel other than what you accepted, let him be eternally condemned!" (Galatians 1:8-9). The Bible clearly teaches that any group that teaches a different view of salvation and of Jesus than that presented in the Bible is a non-Christian movement. It is not just "another way to God." While Jesus loves all people, his teachings clearly contradict those of Mormonism. Further, if God is love, he would not lead people to create different religions that contradict each other. Rather, he would give us one way and mark it clearly. He did so in the Bible, which is affirmed by fulfilled prophecies about the Messiah and Jesus' resurrection from the dead.

Communicating with Mormons

If you don't already know someone who is a Mormon, you probably will in the future. With the rapid growth of Mormonism in North America, it is important to have some understanding of what they believe—especially if you are a Christian. You may find the following suggestions helpful in making connections in your conversations:

- *Pray:* God's wisdom serves as the foundation for all meaningful communication.

- *Build a Relationship:* You don't have to become best friends, but it's difficult to find someone willing to listen to your story if you don't care enough to listen to theirs.

- *Ask Questions:* How did you become involved in Mormonism? What are your thoughts about Jesus? What is your understanding of the New Testament?

- *Share Your Story:* Once you've built a relationship and asked some questions, take a moment to share how Jesus has changed your life.

- *Provide Resources:* A contemporary translation of the Bible, Christian music the person may like, or even this book can help open further opportunities to discuss the Jesus of the New Testament.

This concludes our discussion about Mormonism. Now let's turn our attention to another alternative religion in America that has also grown rapidly in size and significance. Even newer than Mormonism, this religious movement already has some six million members worldwide. Turn the page and read on as we take a look at the the big deal about Jehovah's Witnesses.

What's with the

6 | # Watchtower?

S ince their beginning in 1872, the Jehovah's Witnesses have grown rapidly into one of the largest and most influential religious groups in America today. Whether through door-to-door efforts, missionary service, or local Kingdom Hall work, millions of members focus devoted attention toward personal improvement and the expansion of their faith to people of all backgrounds. To get some idea of their impact, here are some key statistics:

- There are over 6.6 million Jehovah's Witnesses worldwide.

- Over 247,000 new members were baptized into the movement in 2005.

- Nearly 100,000 congregations have been started, with 12,261 locations in the United States.

- One out of every 282 Americans is a Jehovah's Witness.[1]

In America, many Kingdom Hall buildings dot the landscape. The average passerby may easily mistake the facility as just another church without any awareness of the vast differences between Jehovah's Witnesses and Christianity. In this chapter we'll review some basic facts that consider the movement's history, writings, beliefs, and social controversies. I (John) have interviewed and debated practicing Jehovah's Witnesses as well as leaders who formerly worked at the Jehovah's Witnesses headquarters in Brooklyn and later left when they discovered their movement is at odds with the Bible.

What's with the Knocking?

You've probably had a Jehovah's Witness knock on your door before. They seem very sincere and carry around a Bible just like a Christian. The question is, why?

According to their beliefs, door-to-door witnessing is one of the most important steps in attaining their salvation. Carrying out this task enables them to fill up a key part of their checklist of things to do to reach heaven.

The Origins of the Jehovah's Witnesses

The early history of the Jehovah's Witness movement is heavily marked by the activities of its first three leaders. Let's take a quick tour together through the eyes of these leaders.

The Founder: Charles T. Russell

The founder, Charles Taze Russell, was born on February 16, 1852 in Old Allegheny, Pennsylvania. His parents were members of the Allegheny City Congregational Church, which he also attended. In 1868, when challenged on his views of hell, Russell expressed doubts about eternal torment. The following year, he abandoned his church and the Bible.

Russell attended a religious meeting in 1870 and heard Jonas Wendell, a Second Adventist, speak. From Wendell he was informed that man does not have a soul and that unbelievers, upon death, are simply annihilated. This provided a resolve to his doubt and dislike of the doctrine regarding eternal punishment.

Two years later Russell organized a Bible class to promote his views and later met N.H. Barbour in 1877, who believed in the invisible return of Christ. Russell, who claimed he had already come to the same conclusion, now began to promote this view. Russell began publishing *Zion's Watch Tower and Herald of Christ's Presence* in 1879, and founded Zion's Watch Tower Tract Society in 1884.

By 1888, Russell's staff had grown to 50 people, and he had a seven-volume series of books as well as a growing magazine. In his writings he predicted that God's judgment would occur by 1914 and usher in the millennial age. When that didn't happen, some people left the movement. But because World War I started in the same year, many thought Russell was close and that the prophecy would soon be fulfilled. Any prophecies that turned out wrong were adjusted as the movement grew—until Russell's death in 1916.

The Communicator: Joseph Franklin Rutherford

Joseph Rutherford assumed the organization's leadership after Russell's death and expanded its influence through further publications. In addition to several books, Rutherford promoted many new communication methods that helped spur tremendous growth during his years of leadership. These included:

- Radio broadcasts: Over 400 radio stations carried broadcasts featuring the teachings of the Jehovah's Witnesses.

- Door-to-door outreach: Rutherford expanded the organization's efforts to reach new converts.

- *Awake!* magazine: He began this second magazine, which provided a popular format for reaching additional readers with the Watchtower message.

- A new name: Under Rutherford's influence, the movement changed its name to the Jehovah's Witnesses to separate themselves from Christian denominations.

The Innovator: Nathan H. Knorr

After Rutherford's death in 1942, Nathan H. Knorr took over as the organization's new leader. Knorr got off to a difficult start because of several legal issues that involved the Jehovah's Witnesses and the World War II military draft, freedom of speech, and freedom of worship.

Resilient, Knorr helped found a missionary school for the purpose of spreading the message of the Jehovah's Witnesses worldwide. In addition, he helped in the efforts to publish the New World Translation of the Bible now used as the official Bible translation of the movement. With the help of more advanced technology and travel, the movement quickly accelerated from around 100,000 members to over two million members worldwide during his 35 years of leadership.

Who's the Boss?

Jehovah's Witnesses are definitely a top-down type of organization. The organization is said to be modeled after the early Christian church. The basic principle is that all baptized men have the opportunity to become ministerial servants or elders and lead the Christian congregation. The international organization is led by a governing body headquartered in Brooklyn, New York. Each congregation is led by congregational elders, whose appointment is recommended by traveling representatives of the Governing Body to a branch office. Ministerial servants assist the elders (see endnote for more details on organizational structure).[2]

The New World Translation and Other Publications

Jehovah's Witnesses are quite prolific when it comes to writing. Even as a nonprofit organization, the Watchtower Society ranked as one of the top 40 revenue-making publishers in New York. With over 60 million magazines printed per month along with millions of copies of books, brochures, and scriptures printed each year, an enormous amount of material exists for the devoted.

The New World Translation of the Holy Scriptures

The New World Translation (NWT) of the New Testament was released in 1950, and the complete Bible became available in 1961. This is a modern translation of the Bible, yet it contains many inaccuracies. The NWT clearly shows its bias for the use of the word

Jehovah—it includes nearly 7000 uses of the word in the Old Testament (far more than the literal number of times the Hebrew word is used). In the New Testament of the Bible, the Greek equivalent of *Jehovah* is not used at all, but the NWT uses a speculative theory to include it 237 times.

Then there's the translation of "torture stick" in place of "cross" (Jehovah's Witnesses argue Jesus was hung on a pole rather than a cross), the translation of the words usually listed as "hell" with their original language equivalents (such as *gehenna* or *sheol*), and the infamous mistranslation of John 1:1 (where "the Word"—Jesus—is translated as "a god" rather than "the Word was God"). The names of the members of the translation team that produced the NWT have mostly remained hidden, but Bill and Joan Cetnar, who worked in the Brooklyn headquarters, have revealed some important information about the translation work on the NWT.

F.W. Franz, along with then-president Nathan Knorr, headed the secret committee of seven translators. Franz was asked questions in a court case in Edinburgh, Scotland, and the *Scottish Daily Express,* on November 24, 1954, reported his testimony word for word. Franz, under oath, stated that 1) he and Knorr had the final word in translation; 2) he (Franz) was head of the society's publicity department; 3) translations and interpretations came from God, invisibly communicated to the publicity department by angels of various ranks who control[ed] the translators.[3] These statements by the leaders and translators concerning the accuracy of their New World Translation is evidence that they are in agreement with the Watchtower's claim to be God's sole channel of communication on earth. But Franz also admitted under oath that he could not read Greek or Hebrew, the original languages of the Bible.

John 1:1 in the New World Translation

The late Dr. Bruce Metzger, professor of New Testament language and literature at Princeton Theological Seminary and author of *The Text of the New Testament,* examined the Jehovah's Witnesses translation of John 1:1 and wrote:

It must be stated quite frankly that, if the Jehovah's Witnesses take this translation seriously, they are polytheists. In view of the additional light which is available during this age of Grace, such a representation is even more reprehensible than were the heathenish, polytheistic errors into which ancient Israel was so prone to fall. As a matter of solid fact, however, such a rendering is a frightful mistranslation. It overlooks entirely an established rule of Greek grammar which necessitates the rendering, "...and the Word was God."[4]

He should know. Metzger served as one of the major editors of the Greek New Testament used for today's English Bible translations.

The Watchtower claims that its translation of the Bible is the most accurate or one of the most accurate translations yet produced. In *All Scripture Is Inspired by God and Beneficial*, it claims precise grammatical accuracy in translation: "...the *New World Translation*...is *accurate and reliable...a faithful translation of God's word*."[5]

In the New World Translation itself, the Watchtower claims it has translated the Scriptures "as accurately as possible," with both a fear of and love for God—indeed with a great "sense of solemn responsibility.[6]

In *The Kingdom Interlinear Translation of the Greek Scriptures,* the Watchtower claims that its New Testament translation accurately renders "what the original language says and means" and that it does so without bias.[7] The Watchtower Society has even gone so far as to say that God Himself has supervised its translation of the Bible by "angels of various ranks who controlled" the translators.

But what do recognized Greek scholars say about the accuracy of the NWT? Greek scholars, both Christian and non-Christian, have universally rejected the NWT, calling it biased and inaccurate. Dr. Julius Mantey, Greek scholar and author of the *Hellenistic Greek Reader* and *A Manual Grammar of the Greek New Testament,* not only rejected the NWT, but also publicly demanded that the society stop misquoting his *Grammar* to support it. Of the NWT translation he wrote:

> I have never read any New Testament so badly translated as *The Kingdom Interlinear Translation of the Greek*

Scriptures. In fact, it is not their translation at all. Rather, it is a distortion of the New Testament. The translators used what J. B. Rotherham had translated in 1893, in modern speech, and changed the readings in scores of passages to state what Jehovah's Witnesses believe and teach. That is *distortion,* not translation.[8]

Clearly, those who really want to know what God said in the 66 books of the Bible should consult translations of the Bible written by known and trustworthy scholars.

The Watchtower

The Watchtower magazine is the foundational resource of the movement, now available in 158 languages worldwide. Over 28 million copies of each issue are printed and are used for both teaching and outreach efforts.[9] Its purpose, stated inside the cover of the magazine, is this:

> The purpose of *The Watchtower* is to exalt Jehovah God as Sovereign Lord of the universe. It keeps watch on world events as these fulfill Bible prophecy. It comforts all peoples with the good news that God's Kingdom will soon destroy those who oppress their fellowmen and that it will turn the earth into a paradise. It encourages faith in God's now-reigning King, Jesus Christ, whose shed blood opens the way for mankind to gain eternal life. *The Watchtower,* published by Jehovah's Witnesses continuously since 1879, is nonpolitical. It adheres to the Bible as its authority.

Interestingly, its workers and editors are volunteers who both live and work in the magazine office community complex in Brooklyn, New York. This magazine has been called the voice of the movement and serves as the key publication for members.

Awake!

Awake! is a general-interest magazine published by the Jehovah's

Witnesses. It is considered a companion magazine to *The Watchtower,* which focuses mostly on Bible study and doctrine. *Awake!* has a wider scope and publishes articles on science, nature, and geography, usually with a religious slant.[10] As of 2007, the publication has a circulation of over 34 million copies per month in 81 languages.

Other Publications

In addition to the above resources, followers can find an entire bookstore of resources through the Watchtower, including titles such as *What Does the Bible Really Teach?, The Secret of Family Happiness, The Greatest Man Who Ever Lived,* and *How Can Blood Save Your Life?*[11]

Watchtower Theology

While some Jehovah's Witnesses teachings appear similar to those found in traditional Christianity, several foundational beliefs exclude this movement from being a part of biblical, orthodox Christianity. The most obvious differences include the following:[12]

God

- His only appropriate name is Jehovah (of course, the Bible lists several names for God, not just this one).

- Jehovah is all-powerful and all-knowing, but He is not omnipresent. God is spoken of as having a location. His throne is in heaven.

- God exists, but he is not Triune (one in essence, three in person). Jesus was a created being, not God over all creation. The Holy Spirit is simply a force.

Creation

- Jehovah created all things of his own power out of nothing (*ex nihilo*).

- Jehovah's first creation was Jesus Christ, through whom he created all other things.

Jesus

- In his pre-human state Jesus was the archangel Michael, the first created being. He was also called the Logos, "the second greatest personage of the universe."

- In his human state he was nothing more than a perfect human being.

- In his posthuman state he was recreated as a glorious immortal spirit creature, ascended into heaven, and is now the head under Jehovah of God's capital organization over the entire universe. Jehovah's Witnesses teach that Jehovah God raised Jesus from the dead, but his resurrection was not a physical, bodily resurrection. Furthermore, the Watchtower writes that Jesus did not take his human body to heaven and says that Jesus will not return to earth in human form.

Salvation

- What does a Jehovah's Witness need to do to go to heaven? He has to do more than merely accept the kingdom message. He must take in knowledge, believe in the Jesus Christ of the Watchtower, repent, dedicate himself to Jehovah, recognize the Watchtower Society as God's authoritative organization on Earth, conduct his life in harmony with the teachings and activities of the Watchtower Society, maintain integrity to Jehovah and to his earthly organization, and then endure faithfully to the end.

- Not everyone goes to heaven. According to Jehovah's Witnesses, there are two classes of saved people. The first group is "the Congregation of God," which consists of only 144,000 people out of all the people who have ever lived on Earth (also called the Remnant). These are also called the "little flock" of Luke 12:32 and the "faithful and wise servant" of Matthew 24:45. Only these people who have a heavenly calling can hope to live and reign with Christ in heaven. If you are part of this special 144,000 who get to go to heaven, it might separate you forever from other family members who remain on planet Earth and are part of the second group.

The second group is "the Great Crowd." These are the "other sheep" of John 10:16 and the "great multitude" of Revelation 7:9. They have only an earthly hope; their hope is to live on a restored paradise Earth.

- After death, a person who is a Jehovah's Witness will go to heaven (one of the above two classes). All others will cease to exist. They become nothing and are annihilated.

How Does It Work?

Each week, Jehovah's Witnesses are expected to participate in five hours of meetings that include a two-hour Sunday gathering, a one-hour weekly meeting (usually on Tuesdays), and another two-hour meeting during the week for Bible study and outreach training.

Social and Ethical Issues

Every religion has its own list of do's and don'ts, but Jehovah's Witnesses stand out because of some unique social and ethical positions among their distinctives. Interestingly, they claim to base these positions on their interpretation of their Bible and argue that anyone who claims to believe the Bible will arrive at their conclusion.

Among the most controversial practices or positions are...

Refusal to Observe Birthdays

Jehovah's Witnesses disagree with the celebrating of birthdays because they give excessive attention to individuals. They reason that all attention belongs to Jehovah. Interestingly, part of the reasoning behind this belief is that the only two birthday parties mentioned in the Bible involved unbelievers and execution.[13]

The official pronouncement of the Jehovah's Witnesses states, "The early Christians did not celebrate birthdays. The custom of celebrating birthdays comes from ancient false religions. True Christians give gifts and have good times together at other times during the year."[14] There is not much biblical evidence to support the claim, but that's their view.

Did You Know...

...that former U.S. president Dwight D. Eisenhower, tennis champions Venus and Serena Williams, Michael Jackson, and the musical artist Prince have each been members of the Jehovah's Witnesses at some point in their lives? Find out which other celebrities have been among the followers of this religion at http://www.adherents.com/largecom/fam_jw.html.

Refusal to Observe Christmas and Easter

Even Jesus' birthday is not observed. According to the Watchtower, "Jesus never commanded Christians to celebrate his birth...Christmas and its customs come from ancient false religions. The same is true of Easter customs, such as the use of eggs and rabbits. The early Christians did not celebrate Christmas or Easter, nor do true Christians today."[15]

In contrast, the Bible reveals that Jesus celebrated the Jewish holidays, including Passover (Matthew 26:18), Purim (John 5), and Hanukkah (John 10:22). Clearly, Jesus did not view holidays as evil, since he participated in these celebrations. Further, the Bible claims that he never sinned. In addition, early Christian history notes that Christians have celebrated the resurrection date (Easter) since the beginning of the Christian movement. The celebration of Christ's birth has been observed for hundreds of years as well, with written references to this tradition as early as the mid-fourth century.

Refusal to Observe Other Holidays

As you may have noticed by now, Jehovah's Witnesses aren't a festive bunch. Based on their opposition to excessive eating, Thanksgiving is banned. Also, patriotic holidays are not observed.

Rejection of Patriotic Involvement

Because Jehovah's Witnesses claim they are citizens of Jehovah's kingdom, they refuse to profess allegiance to any other kingdom. This is the basis for their pacifism and their choices to not support the armed forces, not vote, and not salute the flag. Worldwide, Jehovah's Witnesses pursue little political involvement. However, this practice appears at contrast with Jesus' statement to "give to Caesar what is Caesar's, and to God what is God's" (Matthew 22:21).

Rejection of Blood Transfusions

Perhaps most controversial of all is the Jehovah's Witnesses' stance against donating blood or accepting blood transfusions. Based on an interesting interpretation of verses in Leviticus and Acts about animal sacrifices, they believe that anyone who accepts a blood transfusion should be kicked out of the faith.[16]

However, the Bible simply states only that the *eating* of blood was prohibited. This was for health reasons, in addition to the fact that this practice was commonly associated with the pagan religions of the nations surrounding the Israelites. Tragically, hundreds or perhaps even thousands of Witnesses and their children have died needlessly because they have held firm to the Watchtower's unbiblical view.[17]

Conversations with Jehovah's Witnesses

Many of the same basic guidelines for interacting with Mormons can also be used in conversations with Jehovah's Witnesses:

- What does *the Bible* say about who Jesus is? (The Bible you use will make a big difference in this discussion because it's helpful to know what the original biblical languages say.)
- Did Jesus *physically* rise from the dead?

- On what basis does God say he will forgive our sins and give us the gift of eternal life in heaven?

Let's now compare the six foundational beliefs of biblical Christianity with the teachings of Jehovah's Witnesses:

Belief	Jehovah's Witnesses Perspective	Biblical Perspective
God	God is named Jehovah. He lives in heaven, and is seated on his throne (not omnipresent). No acknowledgment of the Trinity.	One God in three persons—Father, Son, and Holy Spirit.
Holy Book	The New World Translation of the Bible, along with *The Watchtower* magazine. *Awake!* magazine and other official Watchtower publications are also highly valued.	The 66 books of the Holy Bible are the sole authoritative works of Christianity.
Sin	The original sin caused humans to inherit death and sin.	All people have sinned (except Jesus).
Jesus Christ	Jesus is God's first creation, the archangel Michael. Denial of the physical resurrection.	God's perfect son, holy, resurrected, divine (second person of the Trinity), yet also fully human.
Salvation	There are two classes of people that will be saved by good works. Each class is working to gain a different salvation (see earlier section on salvation).	Obtained only by God's grace through faith in Jesus Christ, not by human effort.
Afterlife	Jehovah's Witnesses either obtain a form of heaven on Earth or reach special status as one of the 144,000. Non-Jehovah's Witnesses are punished by annihilation at death.	At death, all people will enter heaven or hell based on whether they have salvation in Jesus Christ. There is no annihilation; punishment in hell is eternal.

Jehovah's Witnesses hold a belief system that is distinctly different from biblical Christianity. They follow different views of who God is, who Jesus is, what books are "from God" (and how they are translated), and how a person obtains salvation. To suggest that Jehovah's Witnesses are Christians is not an accurate statement.

Don't Stop Here!

For additional resources about talking with Jehovah's Witnesses, check out John Ankerberg's *Fast Facts on Jehovah's Witnesses* or Herbert Kern's *How to Respond to Jehovah's Witnesses*. Several articles about this religious group can also be found at www.johnankerberg.org.

Mormonism and Jehovah's Witnesses are among the largest two alternative religions in American culture today. There is now another spiritual movement that has attracted much attention in recent years, especially among today's teenagers. According to some studies, this is the fastest growing religious group in America in terms of percentage of growth.

Is Witchcraft for Real?

7

"Wicca is the fastest-growing religion in America, and the number of Wiccans is doubling every two years or so."[1]

"The 2001 American Religious Identification Survey estimated that at least 134,000 adults identified themselves as Wiccans in the US."[2]

"The Wiccan community is growing at an exceptional rate, and is projected to be the Third Largest religion by 2012."[3]

From Harry Potter to films such as *The Craft* to today's top video games, witchcraft has grown into a top-selling media issue. Many believe the popularity of such films and games has spurred the growth of the popular movement most commonly known as Wicca.

Is Wicca really that popular? With titles such as *Wicca: A Guide for the Solitary Practitioner* (400,000+ copies sold) now reaching bestseller status, Wicca's acceptance can be seen everywhere from public schools to the U.S. military, infiltrating both local bookstores and local churches.

Wicca is often introduced as a natural part of everyday life. For instance, one book on Wicca begins by stating, "Chances are that witches have been part of your life from as far back as you can remember. These were the homely, wart-nosed crones who tried to turn children into a snack, poisoned apples, and imprisoned beautiful princesses."[4] From this common negative perception the transition is made to introduce Wicca in a positive light, along with its rituals and beliefs.

In our conversation together in this chapter, we'll take a moment to define Wicca as presented in today's culture, briefly tour its history, share its primary beliefs and rituals, and review how Wicca is distinctly different from Christianity as a religion.

What Is Wicca?

Defining *Wicca* is somewhat difficult. According to Wiccan writers, Wicca can be defined in different ways:

- "These days, Wicca refers to a set of practices, beliefs and traditions associated with people who call themselves witches."[5]

- "What exactly is Wicca? For now, let's just say that Wicca is an earth-based or nature-based religion found on ancient beliefs."[6]

- "Wicca is a nature religion. It sees the divine in all things, especially in the natural world, and takes the wonderful diversity that is in nature as its guide, celebrating divinity in all its manifestations."[7]

The common elements these definitions share are these—Wicca is...

1. A nature religion
2. built upon ancient ideas
3. associated with witchcraft.

From these three core identifying marks, Wicca expands to include certain shared beliefs and practices built upon its unique, though not ancient, history.

A Brief History of Wicca

The history of Wicca is highly disputed. Some claim that the religion has its roots in the matriarchal pagan religions of prehistoric Europe. However, modern witchcraft, upon which most of modern Wicca is based, arises from the writings of Gerald Gardner. He joined the New Forest coven in England in 1939, where he remained for several years until the repeal of England's witchcraft laws. Then, concerned that the movement would die out, he published *Witchcraft Today* (1954) and *The Meaning of Witchcraft* (1960).

What Is a Coven?

A coven is a group of witches who practice their religion together. *Coven* probably comes from the Middle English word *covent,* which means "a gathering." The English words *convent* and *convene* come from the same root.[8]

Wicca has developed in several directions since it was first popularized by Gerald Gardner. In *Book of Shadows,* Gardner described the initiation procedures into Wicca. Raymond Buckland introduced modern Wicca to America after moving to Long Island. Although Buckland followed the *Book of Shadows* as he received it from Gardner, when the coven was eventually turned over to Theos and Phoenix, they enlarged the *Book of Shadows,* adding further degrees of initiation that were required before members could found their own covens. Interest grew and the beliefs of the religion spread, by the printed word and word of mouth, faster than the initiatory system was prepared to handle.[9]

Raymond Buckland published several works that helped further the growth of the movement during the 1970s and 1980s. They included *Witchcraft—Ancient and Modern, Witchcraft From the Inside, The Tree: The Complete Book of Saxon Witchcraft,* and *Buckland's Complete Book of Witchcraft* (also known as "Uncle Bucky's Big Blue Book" or simply "The Big Blue Book"), and a workbook that sought to train readers in magical and ritual techniques as well as Wiccan teachings and rituals. Many of the currently popular Wicca books build upon ideas from Buckland's teachings.

On September 4, 1986, in *Dettmer vs. Landon,* a U.S. district court officially sanctioned Wicca as a religion.[10] Several legal cases have been ruled in favor of Wicca since that time, including official acceptance of Wicca within the U.S. armed forces.[11] The first Wiccan wedding to be legally recognized in the United Kingdom was performed in 2004.[12]

Wicca 101

Wicca holds no uniform system of beliefs, yet legally draws heavily on a 1974 list of beliefs developed by the Council of American Witches, called the *Principles of Wiccan Belief.* Simply stated, these beliefs are:

1. Know yourself.
2. Know your Craft.
3. Learn.
4. Apply knowledge with wisdom.
5. Achieve balance.
6. Keep your words in good order.
7. Keep your thoughts in good order.
8. Celebrate life.
9. Attune with the cycle of the earth.
10. Breathe and eat correctly.
11. Exercise the body.
12. Meditate.
13. Honor the Goddess and God.[13]

Other primary Wiccan statements of belief include:

The Wiccan Law

Several versions of this law exist, though this shortened version is widely used. All versions contain both the Wiccan Rede and the Rule of Three.

Bide the Wiccan Law ye must,
In perfect love and perfect trust.
These eight words the Wiccan Rede fulfill,
An ye harm none do as ye will.
And ever mind the Rule of Three,
What ye send out comes back to thee.
Follow this with mind and heart.
And merry ye meet and merry ye part.

The Wiccan Rede

Rede, a Middle English word derived from Old English and Old High German, is thought to mean "advice." If there is any one statement upon which all Wiccans agree, it is the Rede: "an ye harm none do as ye will." The general idea is simply that so long as your actions do not harm another (including the environment), then you are permitted to do whatever you choose.

This conviction nicely complements the politically correct attitude of our culture, which could likewise be stated as, "Do whatever you want unless it hurts someone else." Unfortunately, this belief is not a workable basis for living. For instance, what one person thinks doesn't hurt someone else sometimes *does* hurt other people. A person can also be mistaken about what is good or bad for himself. What is the basis for evaluation? Who is right, and who is wrong?

Biblical Christianity provides solid answers to these questions by its belief that God has revealed the information we need for life through Jesus Christ and through the Bible. Therefore, Christians hold that the Bible is the sole basis and standard for decision-making. Rather than asking whether a particular practice hurts another person or just doing "as ye will," the Bible's standard is to ask whether your actions are pleasing to God, and to show love toward others.

The Rule of Three

The Rule of Three states that "what ye send out comes back to thee." This means essentially that whatever energy you send out in a spell, be it good or bad, will be returned to you threefold, or three times stronger.[14] This rule is often also used in reference to good or bad deeds, meaning that what one does to others, good or bad, will be returned to you three times as much.

This rule is somewhat similar to the Eastern religious concept of karma. And it is not the same as the Bible's exhortation to "do to others what you would have them do to you" (Matthew 7:12, also known as the Golden Rule). Why? Because biblical Christianity teaches that there is a future judgment for sin, and that there are many who do wrong yet still experience good things in this life (Luke 16:19-31). What we experience in this life is not all there is, according to the Bible (Philippians 1:21-23).

Those who suffer in this life for doing good are promised rewards in eternity. The heroes listed in Hebrews 11—such as Abraham, Isaac, Jacob, and Moses—are examples of people who were commended for their faith, yet none of them received in this life the good things promised by God (Hebrews 11:39).

The Wiccan Code of Chivalry

The Wiccan Code of Chivalry (also called the Old Code) is explained as follows:

> That code, as we envision it today, exemplifies a deep love of the Wiccan religion and of those who practice that religion. It is carried forth in some of the wording of an initiation wherein the initiate swears to defend the Lord and Lady [God and Goddess] and all those who love Them, in this life and all those sure to follow.[15]

In Wiccan literature, there is a recurring emphasis in helping those in need and standing up for those less fortunate. Why? As we noted above, if a Wiccan believes that what he or she does returns to them three times stronger, it becomes of great importance to do good to others. This is not simply for the benefit of the other person, but also to help better one's own life by sending out "positive energy" that returns threefold.

The Five Elements

"In Wicca we use a system of five elements from which all existence is derived. These elements are Air, Fire, Water, Earth, and Spirit."[16] Interestingly, these elements are associated with the pentagram symbol.

Is the Pentagram Wiccan?

While the pentagram symbol is not exclusive to Wicca, it is the symbol most commonly associated with Wicca in modern times. It is often circumscribed—depicted within a circle—and is usually (though not exclusively) shown with a single point upward. The inverse pentagram, with two points up, is a symbol of the second degree initiation rite of traditional Wicca. To the right is an example of a pentacle, a Wiccan pentagram enclosed within a circle.[17]

Wiccan Theology

One Wiccan author has noted, "Wicca is a religion that combines two important elements: spirituality and magic."[18] As such, it also holds no consistent theology, though the following presents some basic thoughts on general areas of belief:[19]

- *God:* Contemporary Wiccans worship the Great Mother Goddess and her partner the Horned God (Pan), but these and a host of other pagan deities are said to represent various aspects of an impersonal creative force called "The One" or "The All"—reflecting the current influence of Eastern monism popularized in New Age thought. Wiccans regard all aspects of nature—plants, rocks, planets—as having spirit. This stands in clear contrast with the biblical concept of one God who is creator of all and stands above and apart from his creation.

- *Jesus:* Jesus is seen as an enlightened person or a wizard by some. He is not the Son of God or virgin born.

He was a great prophet or a religious leader, and he did not die for the sins of the world because the concept of sin and Satan does not exist in Wiccan beliefs. Jesus may be viewed positively by some Wiccans, but the Jesus of history is redefined in a way that is false and does not line up with the Bible.

- *Holy Spirit:* Wicca teaches, according to one well-known Wiccan site, that "it really matters little whether we associate with the divine as the 'Father, Son and Holy Ghost' or 'The One, Goddess and God.' Ultimately, the concept is the same." The Holy Spirit is rarely mentioned in Wicca. When it is, the attitude is usually that it is just one of many spirits rather than a unique person of the Trinitarian God as taught in biblical Christianity. Assuming God exists, wouldn't you think his identity is important to him?

- *Sin:* Wiccans essentially believe that as long as no one is hurt, any action is acceptable. As a result, sin is also redefined as acts that hurt others rather than offenses toward a holy God. If God exists, it is important that we understand how our sin positions us with him.

- *Salvation:* "All religions lead in the same direction, simply taking different paths to get there. Witches feel that all should therefore be free to choose their own path."[20] Many paths may sound like a good idea, but this is the polar opposite of Jesus' teaching that he is "*the* way and *the* truth and *the* life" (John 14:6) and that there is only one name by which we can be saved (Acts 4:12). If a friend visits you from another city and calls to get directions to your house, would you tell him, "It doesn't matter which road you take; they all lead to my house"? Of course not! You would give specific directions that would lead to your exact location. Likewise, according to the Bible, not all roads lead to heaven

(Proverbs 14:12). God has provided specific directions for those who want to be with him (John 3:16).

- *Angels:* Most Wiccans do not believe in the Christian form of angels, but rather in beings called "the Watchers." Raven Grimassi describes these "Watchers" as "an ancient race who have evolved beyond the need for physical form."[21] But on what basis or what evidence should we believe Grimassi's arguments?

- *The Afterlife:* Wiccans believe that after one experiences life to its fullest and comes to know and understand every aspect and emotion of life (usually after many reincarnations), their deity will let them into the Summerland. The Summerland also functions as a place of rest between incarnations. As the name entails, it is often envisaged as a place of beauty and peace, where everything people hold close to their hearts is preserved in its fullest beauty for eternity.[22] The concept of hell or eternal punishment, as taught in the Bible, is considered offensive to most Wiccans. On *The John Ankerberg Show*, I (John) once interviewed a heart specialist who had cataloged over 300 near-death experiences , many of which were experiences of hell (see chapter 12). What if you really do need Jesus in order to stay out of hell? Can a person afford to ignore that?

Wicca's Practices and Rituals

Wicca's practices usually revolve around work performed in a Sacred Circle, utilize special and personally created books, and celebrate holidays of the sabbats and esbats.

Magic and Magick

"Is magick with a k different from magic? You bet. Both words come from the same root, meaning 'to be able, to have power,' but magic is what an entertainer does on stage—card tricks, making quarters disappear, sawing a hapless volunteer in half. Magick is the realm of witches and may include spells, healing, the harnessing of psychic forces, and even divination."[23]

The Sacred Circle

The Sacred Circle is the place where most Wiccan rituals and magick is practiced:

> ...most of our ritual workings are done in a special space marked off as a Sacred Circle that is cast in a special way. This circle is purified and designated as a protected space for the practitioners and for whatever deities are invoked during the performance of a rite or ritual.[24]

Special Books

Wicca does not have sacred books comparable to the Bible or Qur'an, but it does make use of the following special books unique to the Wiccan religion:

- *The Mirror Book:* The Mirror Book is essentially a diary, an account of your growth as a witch.[25]

- *The Book of Shadows:* "...is your Craft workbook containing your ritual and spellcraft information. It is your working guide to your written invocations, rites, and spells."[26]

- *Coven Book of Shadows:* "Some covens maintain a Coven Book of Shadows. This Coven Book is usually under the control of the High Priestess, who is responsible for any changes to the contents and for its protection."[27]

Notice that all three books involve people writing their own accounts. In other words, the only special books are those you create on your own. But on what basis can we say that the information you (or others) have recorded should be trusted? Wicca practitioners pass their own words around, but upon whose authority are these words based?

Tools and Instruments Used in Wicca

The following tools are commonly used in Wicca rituals: an altar, altar candles, altar cloth, athame (a double-edged, dark-handled knife), besom (sacred broom), boline (herb-harvesting knife), cauldron (to hold fire), chalice, incense and holder, pentagram symbol, purifying sage, quarter candles, salt container, sword, wand, and water container.[28]

The Eight Sabbats and Esbats

Certain days of the year are important to Wiccans as well. Wiccans typically mark each full moon (and in some cases, new moons) with a ritual called an *esbat*. They also celebrate eight main holidays called *sabbats*. Four of these, the cross-quarter days, are more significant festivals that coincide with old Celtic fire festivals. These are Samhain, May Eve or Beltane, Imbolc, and Lammas. The four lesser festivals are the summer solstice (or Litha) and winter solstice (or Yule), and the spring and autumn equinoxes, sometimes called Ostara and Mabon.[29]

Like Jewish shabbats, Wiccan sabbats begin at sunset the day before the holiday. Four of the sabbats, known as cross-quarter days, have Celtic origins and are called by their Celtic names. The other four mark important points on the solar calendar. The eight sabbats are:

- February 2—Imbolc
- March 21—Ostara (spring equinox)
- May 1—Beltane
- June 22—Midsummer (summer solstice)
- August 2—Lughnasadh
- September 21—Mabon (autumn equinox)
- November 1—Samhain
- December 21—Yule (winter solstice)

Elaborate rituals and magic are typically performed on the esbats, which mark the phases of the moon. The most important esbat is on the full moon, but some groups also recognize esbats of the new moon and the two quarters. Why? Magical power is believed to be especially strong on the night of a full moon, which is why important rituals are usually performed on such nights.

Of great importance to Wicca and other forms of witchcraft is October 31, or Halloween. This day is considered the beginning of the Wiccan year, a time when the veil between the worlds is thin and Wiccans can easily communicate with the spirit world (for more information about this, please see *The Facts on Halloween,* coauthored by John Ankerberg and John Weldon, along with articles at www.johnankerberg.org).

What the Military Says

"Wiccans employ such means as dance, chant, creative visualization and hypnosis to focus and direct psychic energy for the purpose of healing, protecting and aiding members in various endeavors."

—FROM THE U.S. ARMY'S *A HANDBOOK FOR CHAPLAINS,* PP. 231-36

Other Rituals

A Wiccan wedding is called a handfasting—a ritual in which the couple's clasped hands are tied together by a cord or ribbon (hence the phrase "tying the knot"). Divorces are sometimes observed with a handparting, a ritual in which the couple may jump over a broom before parting.[30]

Some Wiccans also observe a ritual called a Wiccaning, analogous to a christening for an infant, the purpose of which is to present the infant to the God and Goddess for protection.

The Bible forbids Christian involvement in these types of practices. Deuteronomy 18:10-14 states:

Let no one be found among you who sacrifices his son or daughter in the fire, who practices divination or sorcery, interprets omens, engages in witchcraft, or casts spells, or who is a medium or spiritist or who consults the dead. Anyone who does these things is detestable to the LORD, and because of these detestable practices the LORD your God will drive out those nations before you. You must be blameless before the LORD your God. The nations you will dispossess listen to those who practice sorcery or divination. But as for you, the LORD your God has not permitted you to do so.

God specifically calls the practices described within Wicca as detestable to himself, meaning that they completely contrast his intended desires for those who claim to follow him.

Is Wicca Compatible with Christianity?

The Bible clearly teaches that witchcraft, whether Wiccan or any other form, is detestable to God. He has always commanded his followers to completely avoid its practices.

Wiccan author and authority Scott Cunningham has claimed, "All religions have one ideal at their core: to unite their followers with Deity. Wicca is no different."[31] He also wrote, "Perhaps it's not too strong to say that the highest form of human vanity is to assume that your religion is the only way to Deity."[32] But is it really true that there are many ways to God?[33]

Although it's quite common to hear such reasoning today, when we compare the beliefs of Wicca with those of biblical Christianity, there are substantial fundamental differences regarding who God is. So it cannot be said that the two religions are among those that "have one ideal."

Wiccans generally believe in the essential divinity of humanity. According to Raven Grimassi, "Everything bears the 'divine spark' of its creator."[34] He also claims, "Souls are like brain cells in the mind of the Divine Creator, individual entities and yet part of the whole."[35] There doesn't seem to be any clear distinction in Wicca between humanity and deity. This explains why one proponent could confidently declare,

"There is nothing to be saved from...no God outside the world to be feared and obeyed."[36]

Obviously, if you are divine (of God himself), then you don't have to fear what you do as God. But what if there is only one true God in the universe, and *it is not you?*

According to biblical Christianity, we are created by God and, at death, have to give an account for how we lived our lives. The Bible says God so loved us that he gave his only son on our behalf, that whoever believes in him will not perish but have eternal life (John 3:16). How will God feel if you turn down what he has done?

Here's the bottom line: Is there one true God, or are there a number of deities and a host of demigods? Wicca and Christianity cannot both be true because of their contradictory beliefs. As writer Michael Gleghorn writes:

> It's therefore interesting to note Charlotte Allen's observation: "*In all probability, not a single element of the Wiccan story is true.* The evidence is overwhelming that Wicca is...a 1950s concoction...of an English civil servant and amateur anthropologist" named Gerald Gardner. But surely such questionable historical origins cast doubt on the truth of Wiccan religious beliefs as well. Christianity, however, is firmly rooted in the historical reality of Jesus of Nazareth, whose claim to be the *only* way to God was clearly vindicated when God "furnished proof to all men by raising Him from the dead."[37]

As we compare Wicca with Christianity, we find many significant contrasts:

Belief	Wiccan Perspective	Biblical Perspective
God	Wiccans believe in the God and the Goddess. Many also worship additional pagan deities.	One God in three persons— Father, Son, and Holy Spirit.

Holy Book	Rather than revealed scriptures, Wicca's special books include The Mirror Book, The Book of Shadows, and Coven Book of Shadows.	The 66 books of the Holy Bible are the sole authoritative works of Christianity.
Sin	Do not believe in original sin. Right and wrong are relative concepts based on the Wiccan Rede of "an ye harm none do as ye will."	All people have sinned and are born with a sin nature (except Jesus).
Jesus Christ	Jesus is not sinless, born of a virgin, nor God's son. Some view him as a wizard or enlightened person, but nothing more.	God's perfect son, holy, resurrected, divine (second person of the Trinity), yet also fully human.
Salvation	Salvation is not necessary. Wiccans are encouraged to choose their own path rather than any one particular way of salvation.	Obtained only by God's grace through faith in Jesus Christ, not by human effort. Jesus teaches there is only one way to heaven (John 14:6; Acts 4:12).
Afterlife	Wicca teaches repeated reincarnations rather than death as final. Some Wiccans speak of the Summerland, a resting place for spirits that are finished with reincarnation.	At death, all people will enter heaven or hell based on whether they have salvation in Jesus Christ. The Bible does not support the concepts of reincarnation or the Summerland.

In addition to these contrasts, the Bible singles out witchcraft as something Christians are to avoid. Scripture condemns spiritism (Deuteronomy 18:9-12; 2 Chronicles 33:2-3,6), various forms of sorcery and divination (Exodus 22:18; Deuteronomy 18:9-12; Isaiah 29:8-9; 44:25; Ezekiel 21:21; Hosea 4:12) astrology (Deuteronomy 17:2-5; 2 Kings 17:15-17; Isaiah 47:9-14), and magic (Isaiah 47:9,12; Acts 13:8; 19:16-19). God warns all people, in the strongest words, not to participate in the practices associated with Wicca. For a more complete biblical evaluation of these practices, see the appendix, "Biblical Warnings Against Occult Involvement."

But what if you have participated in witchcraft? God still loves you. The warnings he gives in the Bible are for your safety and good. God wants to protect you from contact with spiritual powers and entities that are deceitful, more powerful than you, and able to blind you spiritually to the true things of God.

If God didn't love you, he wouldn't have gone to such great lengths to warn you about specific practices and philosophies. He desires for you to understand who Jesus is and what he can do for you, both in this life and the next. But you need to investigate Jesus right away because you don't know how much time you have. God is loving, but he is also holy and righteous. As C.S. Lewis noted in The Chronicles of Narnia, Aslan (the lion who represents Jesus) is walking away on the beach when we are told:

> "He'll be coming and going," he had said. "One day you'll see him and another you won't. He doesn't like being tied down—and of course he has other countries to attend to. It's quite all right. He'll often drop in. Only you musn't press him. He's wild, you know. Not like a tame lion."[38]

God is good, but he is also just. He is not tame. Moses recorded it this way: "Just as it pleased the LORD to make you prosper and increase in number, so it will please him to ruin and destroy you. You will be uprooted from the land you are entering to possess" (Deuteronomy 28:63). Why? Because God delights in carrying out his moral judgments just as much as he delights in giving loving rewards.

Can our decisions grieve God? Yes. The people who lived in the days of Noah grieved the Lord and were ultimately destroyed in the flood, yet Noah and his family were saved. Though we have all grieved God, he lovingly invites all people, including you, to come to him, find forgiveness, and receive power to walk in his ways.

Though Wicca has become very popular today, its teachings contradict the beliefs and practices of biblical Christianity. That's why it doesn't make sense to seek ways in which these two religions are compatible.

In the next chapter, we'll investigate another ancient religious system that has grown more popular in Western culture. It has attracted noted celebrities and influenced millions through its writings and seminars. What religion is it? Join us as we dialogue about the growing impact of Kabbalah.

Kabbalah:

A Mystical
8 | # Judaism?

"I wouldn't say studying Kabbalah for eight years...falls under the category of being a fad or a trend. Now there might be people who are interested in it because they think it's trendy, but I can assure you that studying Kabbalah is actually a very challenging thing to do. It requires a lot of work, a lot of reading, a lot of time, a lot of commitment and a lot of discipline."

—POP SINGER MADONNA TO CNN'S RICHARD QUEST[1]

"When I split with Nick [Carter] I coped by going straight to the Kabbalah Centre in Los Angeles, told everyone about the break-up and got a new [red string Kabbalah] bracelet. I go there regularly—it helps me deal with my life."

—PARIS HILTON[2]

K abbalah has reached new levels of popularity in recent years, thanks to a surge of celebrities converting to the faith. Madonna, Paris Hilton, Demi Moore, Roseanne Barr, Britney Spears, Jeff Goldblum, Ashton Kutcher, Guy Ritchie, and Elizabeth Taylor have all reportedly joined in (at least for a period of time) with the movement's growing number of followers.[3] So what is Kabbalah?

Kabbalah claims to be a mystical way of interpreting the Torah, the primary Jewish scriptures, and of attempting to understand God. Practitioners believe the study of Kabbalah can help a person understand the secrets of the universe. *Kabbalah* literally means "that which is received." The teachings of Kabbalah, at first not written down, were supposedly passed directly by word of mouth from teacher to student. This brings us to a key question: Who told the first teacher these secret teachings? Why should we believe the claim that this information helps a person understand the secrets of the universe?

According to the Kabbalah Centre, Kabbalah

> contains the long-hidden keys to the secrets of the universe as well as the keys to the mysteries of the human heart and soul. Kabbalistic teachings explain the complexities of the material and the nonmaterial universe, as well as the physical and metaphysical nature of all humanity. Kabbalah shows in detail how to navigate that vast terrain in order to remove every form of chaos, pain, and suffering.[4]

In the rest of this chapter, we'll navigate through the complexities of Kabbalah by attempting to define this religious movement, describing its history, reviewing its beliefs, and providing a Christian basis for evaluation.

Defining Kabbalah

"Kabbalah does not lend itself to a straightforward definition or even a clear-cut history...it teaches us about the mysteries of life, how the creation works, where we are going, and how we get there."[5]

"Above all, Kabbalah is a meditation on creation, an attempt to find adequate language to describe all that we experience."[6]

From the start, it is difficult to define Kabbalah because of its mysterious history and basis. As a religion, it attempts to historically connect with Judaism, though Orthodox Jews reject the association. As a movement, it truly stands alone in its own beliefs. It lacks a centralized leadership and set of creeds, and as such, defines itself in a more fluid sense. From leading Kabbalists we learn that Kabbalists place their primary emphasis upon experiencing God personally through reading Jewish writings such as the Torah and adding to it their methodology for personal enlightenment.

The History of Kabbalah

Though the history of Kabbalah is said to connect with the creation of the universe, its actual growth as a movement began during the height of medieval times. Kabbalism formally began in Spain, spread throughout Palestine and Europe, and emerged in the past century in the United States through the development of the Kabbalah Centre.

How It All Began

Kabbalism, as a religion, grew out of Jewish tradition and flowered in Provence and the Rhine Valley in the 1100s, with roots extending at least as far away as Palestine and Babylonia and back in time to the second century of the Common Era. Using their mystical methodology, Kabbalists sought to explain how the universe was created (and how it will end), how God is manifested in creation, and how to experience the divine presence for oneself. By the 1200s the center of Kabbalism was located in Spain, where the great book of Zohar was "discovered." After Ferdinand and Isabella of Spain expelled the Jews in the 1490s, Palestine became another center of Kabbalism, especially the town of Safed in Galilee, where the great Rabbi Isaac Luria taught.

Kabbalah Heats Up

By the seventeenth century, Kabbalah was spreading so quickly that some contemplated it would someday replace standard Jewish theology. But in the second half of that century it suffered a major setback when a brilliant 20-year-old Kabbalistic rabbi known as Nathan of Gaza (1643–1680) was forced to choose between death or conversion to Islam. He chose to convert, which devastated many of his followers.

By the eighteenth century, most of organized Judaism began to distance itself from this exotic expression of mysticism. Historians suggest that Kabbalah, as a movement, slowed from that time until the Jewish Renewal movement in America in the 1960s, which opened the door for the resurgence of interest in Kabbalah today.

Kabbalah Today

A modern revival of Kabbalah has been initiated at the controversial Kabbalah Centre, which was founded by Philip Berg in Los Angeles in 1984. The center is run by Philip and his sons, Yehuda and Michael. With a number of branches worldwide, the group has managed to attract many non-Jews, including the entertainment celebrities we noted earlier.

Members look to the Kabbalah Centre as a spiritual organization that teaches the principles of Kabbalah in a unique and user-friendly system accessible to anyone regardless of religion, race, or gender. The Kabbalah Centre hosts Jewish and non-Jewish teachers and students. This is one reason it is not supported by Jewish religious culture. Jewish organizations frequently refer to it as non-Jewish and often consider participation by Jews as problematic because classical Judiasm forbids Jews from participating in religious rituals with non-Jews.

What Is the Red String?

Celebrities such as Demi Moore, Madonna, Winona Ryder, and others wear a braided Kabbalah bracelet made out of red string, which they are told will protect them from the evil eye, defined by the Kabbalah Centre as "the unfriendly stare and unkind glances we sometimes get from the world around us." Supposedly the evil eye is a superstition, a sort of curse, that comes upon a person when the eye of an envious person comes upon you.

According to the Kabbalah Centre:

> Worn around the left wrist, the Red String works in the same way
> as the vaccines of modern medicine. When we receive a vaccination
> against a disease, a weakened strain of the illness is integrated into the
> vaccine. Spiritual immunizations are based on a similar principle. Kab-
> balah teaches that colors have specific frequencies and energies. Red,
> for example, is the color of danger. By binding a Red String to ourselves
> in a very specific manner, we shield ourselves against the dangerous
> negativity that might be directed our way—a spiritual vaccine against the
> destructive forces of the Evil Eye.[7]

Kabbalah Beliefs

Kabbalah emerged out of Judaism and therefore, in its traditional
form, refers back to many Jewish customs. However, Kabbalah has
distinguished itself from Judaism by adding many non-Jewish beliefs
to its religious system.

Did You Know...

...that originally, tradition stated that a person must reach the age of 40 before
studying Kabbalah? Younger people were not considered to have enough
maturity to become followers. Another early tradition said that only *married
men* of age 40 or over were eligible to study Kabbalah.

Kabbalah's Books: The Torah and the Zohar

Kabbalists hold that the Torah, the first five books of the Jewish
scriptures (authored by Moses), are divinely inspired. But Kabbalah
also adheres to methodology that ultimately leads a person away
from the message God gave in the Torah. According to one leading
Jewish mystic, Ershom Scholem, "[The Torah] does not consist merely
of chapters, phrases, and words; rather is it to be regarded as the
living incarnation of the divine wisdom which eternally sends out
new rays of light."[8] In addition, Kabbalah claims that the interpretation of the Torah is heavily influenced by the Zohar.[9]

What is the Zohar? The Zohar is a commentary on the five books of the Torah, and it was written in Aramaic. While most commentaries interpret the Torah as a narrative and legal work, Kabbalah mystics like to interpret it "as a system of symbols which reveal the secret laws of the universe and even the secrets of God."[10] The Zohar is usually traced back to thirteenth-century Spain. Most scholars believe it was written by Spanish Kabbalist Moses de Leon, though some suggest that it was penned by the second-century sage Rabbi Shimon bar Yochai. The Zohar claims there are symbolic or hidden meanings in the Torah and places a special emphasis on numeric meanings embedded within the text of its pages.

On the surface, this may appear quite creative and intriguing. However, this is not how people interpret other writings in life. For example, suppose your boyfriend or girlfriend or spouse wrote you a love letter. How would you interpret it? Would you approach it in some mystical fashion, seeking to find special interpretations in the numerical values of each word? And in doing so, would you completely miss the message the other person was attempting to communicate?

Other Special Writings in Kabbalah

The Torah and Zohar are the two main texts in Kabbalah, and there are several other special rabbinical writings as well, including the Heichalot, Sefer Yetzirah, Bahir, Sefer Chasidim, and several others.[11]

God Interacts with the World

God interacts with the world through ten manifestations, called emanations and known as the Ten Sefirot. These are called:

Keter—crown	*Tif'eret*—beauty
Hochma—wisdom	*Netzah*—victory
Binah—understanding	*Hod*—awe
Hesed—kindness	*Yesod*—foundation
Gevurah—strength	*Shekhinah* or *Malkhut*—presence

These Ten Sefirot are often represented by a diagram referred to as the Kabbalah tree of life. The Bible, however, denies that God interacts with us or the world through emanations. Instead, he is in charge at all times, and available to all every second of life (Colossians 1:16-20).

Kabbalah's Creation Emphasis

The most basic philosophical belief in Kabbalism is that the world is an emanation of the spiritual essence of God. God, or *Ein Sof,* is infinite and transcendent, and can make no direct contact with finite beings. Emanations are like links on a chain hanging downward. At the top, the links are purely spiritual. But as you descend, each link becomes a little more material. In the middle you have a mixture of spiritual and material. At the bottom, the links are almost all material.

The finite creation came into existence when the *Ein Sof* voluntarily limited himself by allowing himself to become manifest through attributes or emanations (the Ten Sefirot). Each emanation is further removed from the *Ein Sof,* and thus further from God's perfection and transcendence.

These emanations of God are repeated on four descending levels. These realms, according to descent, are called:

- *Atsilut* (the world of the heavens or God himself): The highest world in which we are linked to "the Name" with God himself.

- *Beri'ah* (the world of creation): The world in which God is viewed as a lover desiring mystical union.

- *Yetsirah* (the world of formation): The world in which we relate to God as a father.

- *Asiyah* (the world of material action): The world we live in day to day. The inhabitants of this realm relate to God as a subject does to a king, with reverence and awe.

Taking on a personal form, these four levels are also represented as angels serving as intermediaries between God and man.[12]

Kabbalah, then, is similar to Gnosticism, in which a number of lesser spiritual deities bridge the gap between the spiritual deity at the top and man at the bottom. By contrast, biblical Christianity teaches that the Creator himself entered into his creation in the person of Jesus Christ. Because of our sins, we are separated from God. But God has provided his son to be the mediator between us—if we choose to turn from our sin, ask for forgiveness, and enter into a relationship with God. There is only one God, and one mediator between God and man, who is Jesus Christ (1 Timothy 2:5).

The Special Use of Numbers in Kabbalah

Kabbalists believe that the Torah is inspired not just in its obvious interpretations, but also in its numerous hidden meanings. Through the use of symbol interpretation, Kabbalists believe people can find hidden messages in the numerical and alphabetical interpretations of the texts. Further, Kabbalists hold that this mystical system was revealed by God at the same time as the Torah, and that each letter in the Torah has an underlying, secret significance.[13] But the problem with such a claim is that people can subjectively interpret texts in a variety of ways and come up with whatever meaning they want.

As early as the first century B.C., some Jews believed the Torah contained encoded messages and hidden meanings. *Gematria* is one method for discovering hidden meanings in the Torah. Its premise is that each letter in Hebrew also represents a number (such as A=1, B=2). By converting the letters to numbers, Kabbalists believe they can find hidden meanings in the text of the Torah. This method of interpretation has been used extensively by various Kabbalist schools throughout history. Yet different schools have assigned different numerical values to the same letters. This, obviously, changes the outcome of the interpretative process.

Gematria in Practice

One of the most famous applications of gematria involves the New Testament book of Revelation. When "Nero Caesar" is written in its seven Hebrew consonants, they yield a numerical value of 50+200+6+50+100+60+200. The total? The famous number of the Beast, which is 666 (Revelation 13:18). But is this really significant? It all depends on how a person associates what numerical amount is attached to each letter.[14]

Keep in mind that there is no one fixed way to practice gematria. Some say there are up to 70 different methods. One simple method is this: Each syllable or letter forming a word has a characteristic numeric value (for example, A=1, B=2, etc.). The sum of these numeric tags is the word's "key" (For example, *bad* would be B=2, A=1, D=4, and 2+1+4=7, meaning 7 is the word's "key"). That word may be replaced in the text by any other word having the same key. This means that any other word that also has a numerical total of seven would have an associated meaning with the word *bad*. In this way, completely different or hidden meanings of Scripture may be derived.[15]

But do you really think you could replace *God* with *dog* and find a word with similar significance based on the numerical values of the words? For obvious reasons, many Jews regard gematria as more harmful than helpful. They argue that if the numerical codes are elaborate enough, the interpreter can derive almost any meaning he or she wants from the text.[16]

Numbers in Other Religions

Kabbalah is not the only religion to find spiritual significance in numbers. Islamic mystics (Sufis) and Asian religions have long prescribed special spiritual significance to numbers. But in the Bible, Jesus, the apostles, and the prophets indicated that God's truth is conveyed through the meaning of the words in Scripture rather than through numerical formulas.

What to Do with Kabbalah?

Kabbalists claim to hold to a high view of Scripture, seek God with the emotions in addition to the intellect, and have contributed greatly to humanitarian causes in our world today. It is for these reasons Kabbalah has received more widespread acceptance in modern culture.

But how does Kabbalah compare to biblical Christianity? There are some significant differences. For example, the absence of Jesus in Kabbalah is a denial of the facts of history and of his place as God's Messiah in the Old Testament. There, he is called the Messiah and the Son of God.

Second, the emphasis on secret, hidden messages based on esoteric interpretations of Scripture is more similar to Gnosticism than to Christianity. Christianity believes the message conveyed through the words of the Torah and the rest of Scripture is the message God has given for people to read and apply rather than some special hidden message that has to be deciphered in some way or other.

Here are some main points of conflict:

Belief	Kabbalah Perspective	Biblical Perspective
God	God is called *Ein Sof.* There is no belief in the Trinity.	One God in three persons—Father, Son, and Holy Spirit.
Holy Book	The Torah (the first five books of the Bible) and the Zohar (a mystical commentary on the Torah) are considered the most holy writings.	The 66 books of the Holy Bible are the sole authoritative works of Christianity.
Sin	All people have sinned. However, many Kabbalists do not believe in the concept of original sin (humans are born with a sinful nature).	All people have sinned and are born with a sin nature (except Jesus).
Jesus Christ	Jesus is not seen as the Messiah, God's Son. His resurrection is also denied. He was simply another man, though some consider him a good teacher.	God's perfect son, holy, resurrected, divine (second person of the Trinity), yet also fully human.
Salvation	Salvation is gained by holy living plus faith in God. There	Obtained only by God's grace through faith in

	is no security or promise of salvation because it is based on a combination of God's help and human effort.	Jesus Christ, not by human effort.
Afterlife	God will reward the good and punish the wicked.	At death, all people will enter heaven or hell based on whether they have salvation in Jesus Christ.

Kabbalah holds to a different view of who God is, who Jesus is, which books are holy books, and how a person receives salvation. Thus, a person cannot logically practice both Kabbalah and biblical Christianity.

In many respects, the mysticism of Kabbalah more closely resembles certain elements of many Eastern religions, such as Buddhism and Hinduism. We'll turn to these religions next—religions based on worldviews that are distinctly different from those in the Western world.

Part Four

Eastern Religions

"India has two million gods, and worships them all. In religion all other countries are paupers; India is the only millionaire."

—Mark Twain[1]

U nlike Christianity, Judaism, and Islam, which believe there is only one God, Eastern religions are far more pluralistic in nature. To the Hindu, there are millions of gods. To the Buddhist, God is all and all is God. In both, reality is not real—it just seems that way. Therefore, the struggle in Eastern religions is to understand reality apart from ourselves and to see ourselves as one with everything else.

Sound strange? Not to its followers. In fact, between Hinduism and Buddhism alone there are over one billion adherents. If all you know about Eastern religions is that they believe in reincarnation and practice meditation, the next three chapters should be a big help to you. But chances are, you may already know more of the Eastern religious worldviews than you think. Modern films such as the *Star Wars* series and *The Matrix* trilogy include ideas that come from Eastern religious thought.

While there are many Eastern religions, our discussion will focus primarily on the two largest faiths: Hinduism and Buddhism. Then we'll discuss three of the other major Eastern religions—Taoism, Confucianism, and Shintoism—together in one chapter. As we do, we'll look at the impact these religions are having on our world today. Along the way, we'll see how the beliefs in these religions differ from those in biblical Christianity.

Everything Is One?

9

"Hinduism differs from Christianity and other Western religions in that it does not have a single founder, a specific theological system, a single system of morality, or a central religious organization. It consists of 'thousands of different religious groups that have evolved in India since 1500 B.C.E.'"[1]

D id you know that...

* Hinduism is the world's third largest religion, with over 900 million followers[2]

* over 80 percent of India's population practices some form of Hinduism

* at least one million Hindus live in the United States

Without a unified creed, set of beliefs, or centralized holy city, Hinduism has grown into the world's third largest religion. How can a faith without a unified set of beliefs have such a profound influence? Simply by allowing each person to develop his or her own personal religion around a few common concepts held by all the adherents of that group.

In Hinduism, the big idea is to attain freedom from the world as we see it. We need to disconnect from the material existence around us to understand how we connect with the supposed oneness of the world. A basic premise is that God is all and all is God—also known as pantheism (*pan* meaning "all"; *theism* meaning "God").

So is involvement in Hindu practices simple innocence or something more? While the change of pace from our frantic Western culture is appealing, a closer investigation reveals some concerns about the origins, sacred texts, and beliefs of Hinduism.

Hinduism in Our World

Whether you realize it or not, you most likely have already been influenced by some Hindu beliefs through popular books, television shows, and films. For example, you are probably familiar with the following:

- *Yoga:* Millions of Americans practice this form of exercise, which originates from Hinduism. While most of the religious elements have been removed from the yoga taught in today's health clubs, the origin and basis of yoga was not just to help us shed a few pounds.

- *Karma:* Is your karma good or bad? You may not know yours, but you've at least heard the term *karma* in movies such as *Seven Years in Tibet, Kundun,* and *Little Buddha,* or in television shows such as *My Name Is Earl.*[3]

- *Meditation:* Meditation is not an exclusively Hindu practice, but the cross-legged lotus position with outstretched arms is distinctly Hindu.

The History of Hinduism

The origin of Hindu religious beliefs can be traced back to the Indus Valley civilization that occupied the Indus and Ghagger-Hakra river valleys (now Pakistan and western India) around 4000 to 2200 B.C. While much of Hinduism's history is uncertain, it is clear that around 4000 years ago a developed group of people lived in northwest India. When the light-skinned, nomadic Indo-European tribes from the steppes of Russia and central Asia invaded northern India (circa 1500 B.C.), they brought Vedism with them (an ancient religion that included chanting and sacrifices). Their beliefs mingled with the strong, indigenous Indian beliefs. Religious principles mixed and came to include the Hindu beliefs in reincarnation, multiple gods (polytheism), and the spiritual unity of humanity (monism, "one ultimate reality").[4]

Over time, this mix of religious ideas grew through written texts known as the Vedas. Originally passed down orally, these ideas were written down after 1400 up to 400 B.C. Early Vedic religion was devoted to ritual toward many gods. Later Vedic religion transitioned to pantheism (which teaches that the universe, earth, people, and life are all part of God).

Countries with the Highest Proportions of Hindus Worldwide

Country	Percent	Number
Nepal	89	19,000,000
India	79	780,000,000
Mauritius	52	600,000
Guyana	40	300,000
Fiji	38	300,000
Suriname	30	116,000
Bhutan	25	400,000
Trinidad and Tobago	24	300,000
Sri Lanka	15	2,800,000
Bangladesh	11	12,000,000

Source: adherents.com

Hinduism's Sacred Texts

The Hindu scriptures are massive, and, as stated, were written between about 1400 B.C. and 400 B.C. They consist of:

- *The Veda:* The oldest of the Hindu scriptures is the Veda, which literally means "wisdom" or "knowledge." The Vedas contain hymns, prayers, and ritual texts.

The Vedas

The four Vedas are the *Rigveda, Samaveda, Yajuraveda,* and the *Artharvaveda.* They are divided into two parts: the "work" portion (ritual) and the "knowledge" portion (philosophy). This latter portion comprises what is called the Upanishads or Vedant. Because they brought to a close each of the four Vedas, the Upanishads came to be spoken of often as the Vendanta—the *anta* or ends of the Vedas.

The Vedas are mostly a collection of ritualistic hymns to various Hindu gods. The *Rigveda* comprises the foremost collection of these hymns. The *Yajurveda* is a collection of various mantras or special words used to evoke occult power in a negative or positive way. The *Samaveda* combines verses from the *Rigveda* to melodic chants. The *Artharvaveda* is basically a collection of occult spells, incantations, and hymns.[5]

- *The Upanishads:* The Upanishads are a collection of writings composed between 800–600 B.C. Over 100 of them still exist. These writings marked a definite shift from mentions of human sacrifice and magic formulas to mystical ideas about man and the universe. This is particularly noticeable in the idea of the Brahman and the *atman* (the self or soul). The Upanishads came to have a great influence on Gautama Buddha, the founder of Buddhism. As far as the Upanishads themselves are concerned, their vast variety of thought and ideas has allowed a wide variety of views to emerge in their interpretation. That is why the study of the Vedas will not lead to a single viewpoint. In fact, Hindu metaphysicians (religious philosophers) range in their ideas from theism to atheism.

- *The Ramayana:* The Ramayana is one of the two major epic tales of India, the other being the Mahabharata. A sage-poet named Valmiki wrote this tale. The work consists of 24,000 couplets describing the life of Rama, a righteous king who was supposedly an incarnation of the god Vishnu.

- *The Mahabharata:* The Mahabharata is the second epic. It is the story describing the deeds of the Aryan clans and consists of some 100,000 verses composed over an 800-year period beginning about 400 B.C. Contained within this work is a great classic, the Bhagavad Gita, or the "Song of the Blessed Lord."

- *The Bhagavad Gita:* The Bhagavad Gita is the most sacred of all Hindu books and is also the best known and the most read of all Indian works in the entire world. This is despite the fact it was added late to the Mahabharata sometime in the first century A.D. The story in the Bhagavad Gita describes man's duty, which, if carried out, will bring nothing but sorrow. This story has had great impact on Hindu belief in its endorsement of *bhakti,* or devotion to a particular god, as a means of salvation. This concept is taught by Arjuna, the story's main character, when he decides to put his devotion to Vishnu above his own personal desires. The Gita ends with Arjuna devoted to Vishnu and willing to kill his relatives in battle.[6]

Hindu Beliefs

Since Hinduism is not characterized by a unified system of beliefs, the best way to compare it to biblical Christianity is by looking at the main concepts in Hinduism. The two religions differ greatly and force us to ask, "Which is right? Which is true? How can anyone tell whose view of reality is the correct one?"[7]

God

In Hinduism, God (Brahman) is believed to be unknowable, the one impersonal, ultimate, spiritual reality. Sectarian Hinduism personifies Brahman as Brahma (creator, with four heads symbolizing creative energy), Vishnu (preserver, the god of stability and control), and Shiva (destroyer, god of endings). Further, most Hindus worship two of Vishnu's ten mythical incarnations: Krishna and Rama. On special occasions, Hindus may also worship other gods, such as family and individual deities. Hindus claim that there are 330 million gods. In Hinduism, belief in astrology, evil spirits, and curses also prevails.

Biblical Christianity, on the other hand, holds that God is not an unknowable, impersonal divine essence in which our personalities ultimately become an illusion. People do not seek to attain "higher consciousness" so that God and their true self become one. God is not the universe itself, nor is the universe his body (pantheism). God is not the originator of all religions or an eternally hidden deity who is perpetually unknowable, unapproachable, and indescribable (mysticism). God is not monistic, hiding underneath or behind the illusory physical universe.

Among all the religions that have ever existed, the Christian concept of God is entirely unique. It alone adheres to the concept of an infinite, personal Triune God. No other religion has a Trinity. The biblical concept of the Trinity is at once so unexpected and complex and yet so practical that it could never have been invented by people in its biblical form. This one God has revealed that he is three persons, or centers of consciousness, within one Godhead.

Is the God of the Bible knowable? Although he is transcendent and greater than anything we can comprehend, he has revealed who he is, how he created the world, and his moral attributes, such as love, justice, and mercy. He has revealed himself through the prophets in Scripture, and even sent his son Jesus Christ to live among us. When God entered into his creation in the person of Jesus, he used terms we could see and understand. Jesus said, "Anyone who has seen me has seen the Father" (John 14:9), and "I and the Father are one" (John 10:30).

Hinduism flatly rejects such teaching. For example, Swami Nikilananda writes, "It is blasphemy to think that if Jesus had never been born, humanity would not have been saved. It is horrible...never forget the glory of human nature. We are the greatest that ever was or ever will be."[8]

Nikilananda also states, "We are the God of the universe. In worshipping God we have always been worshipping our own self...Let us be God!"[9]

Further, only the God of the Bible speaks to us from before time and out of time. This is a concept Hinduism does not accept. The Bible reveals the following:

> Now this is eternal life: that they may know you, the only true God, and Jesus Christ, whom you have sent. I have brought you glory on earth by completing the work you gave me to do. And now, Father, glorify me in your presence with the glory I had with you *before the world began* (John 17:3-5).

> Father, I want those you have given me to be with me where I am, and to see my glory, the glory you have given me because you loved me *before the creation of the world* (John 17:24, Jesus speaking).

> He chose us in him *before the creation of the world* (Ephesians 1:4).

> *In the beginning, God created* the heavens and the earth (Genesis 1:1).

Ultimately, the Bible challenges all other so-called gods or concepts of God with the words, "To whom will you compare me or count me equal? To whom will you liken me that we may be compared?...I am God, and there is no other; I am God, and there is none like me. I make known the end from the beginning, from ancient times, what is still to come" (Isaiah 46:5,9-10).

Creation

Hindus accept various forms of pantheism and reject the Christian concept of creation, in which God is separate from his creation. According to Hinduism, Brahman alone exists; everything (the universe, earth, man, rocks, animals, fire, etc.) is ultimately an illusion (*maya*). Brahman caused the illusion of creation. There is no beginning or conclusion to creation, only endless repetitions or cycles of creation and destruction. History can have no value because everything is based on an illusion.

If Hinduism is your worldview, you have no explanation as to how or why a person is more important than a cow, a rock, or a drop of water. Everything is an illusion. To say all things are equally important hurts the motivation to fight against disease, hunger, or injustice. One is taught simply to exist.

Humanity

The eternal soul (*atman*) of each human is supposedly a manifestation of Brahman mysteriously trapped in a physical body. A person must live repeated lives or reincarnations, called *samsara*, before the soul can be liberated (*moksha*) from the body. An individual's present life is determined by the law of karma (actions, words, and thoughts in previous lifetimes). The physical body is ultimately an illusion with little inherent or permanent worth. Bodies are generally cremated, and the eternal soul is believed to go to an intermediate state of punishment or reward before rebirth in another body. Rebirths are experienced until one's karma has been removed to allow the soul's reabsorption into Brahman (similar to a drop of water being reabsorbed into the ocean).

By contrast, the God of Christianity says you are important. You were created by him so you could freely choose to know and love him. You were created in the image of God, reflecting some of his attributes, such as a desire to love and to fix injustices. You were created with a sense of eternity in your heart.

Committing Wrongs or Sins

Hinduism does not teach of man's rebellion against a holy God. Ignorance of unity with desire and violation of dharma (social duty) are humanity's problems. Christianity teaches that the problem of sin is rebellion against God's perfect ways. Humans are separated from the presence of God by sin. We stand in need of a Savior who can rescue us from the power of sin in our lives.

Salvation

There is no clear idea or plan of salvation in Hinduism. *Moksha* (freedom from infinite being and selfhood and final self-realization of the truth) is the goal of existence. Yoga and meditation are taught by gurus (religious teachers) and are supposedly ways to attain *moksha*. Hindus hope and strive to eventually leave the cycle of reincarnation, to leave behind the illusion of personal existence and become one with the impersonal god, which is cessation of activity. In contrast, Christianity teaches that your personality, soul, body, and mind are important to God and unique. God desires to have a personal relationship with you, *not* have you become a part of him. In Hinduism, your personality is the problem, an illusion which you must be willing to accept.

Karma's Impact on the Caste System

Many interpret India's caste system in accordance with karma. Through good deeds in this life, a person supposedly has the opportunity for reincarnation in a higher caste. But one will not know if they are successful until they die and are born into a new caste. The negative consequence of believing that you can only be born into a caste is that it robs Hindus of any motivation to attempt moving from one caste system to another in this life or to help someone in a poorer situation rise to a better situation. The result is a religion that generally lacks the desire to help the poor obtain education and a better way of life.

The Ultimate Goal of Hinduism: *Moksha*

The ultimate desire of the Hindu is to reach *moksha,* or a release from the cycle of reincarnation. The word also means "redemption" and serves as the Hindu equivalent of salvation in order to reach nirvana, or the reabsorption of the person with ultimate reality. Hindus believe there are three possible paths to *moksha:*

1. The Way of Activity

The first path to the Hindu release from the cycle of reincarnation is the way of activity, also called *karma yoga*. This is a very popular means of salvation and places emphasis on the idea that liberation may be obtained by fulfilling a person's familial and social duties to overcome the weight of the bad karma one has accumulated. Bruce Bickel and Stan Jantz observe the following:

> On the religious side, a good Hindu will worship gods, goddesses, and spirits through ceremonies that take place both in the temple and at home. The Brahmin priests oversee the worship and ceremonies in the temples, which are often paid for by wealthy Hindus who want to build up good karma.
>
> On the social side, a good Hindu must be very careful to stay within the caste. This means working and marrying within the caste, eating or not eating certain foods, and raising children who will do the same.[10]

2. The Way of Knowledge

The second way of salvation is the way of knowledge, also called *jnana yoga*. The basic premise of the way of knowledge is that the cause of our bondage to the cycle of rebirths is ignorance. According to Hindu teachings, human ignorance consists of the false belief that we are individual selves. This ignorance gives rise to our bad actions, which result in bad karma. Hindu salvation is achieved through reaching a state of consciousness in which we realize this error and concede our identity with Brahman. This is achieved through deep meditation, and is part of the discipline of yoga.

Four stages outline this way of knowledge and involve the leadership of a guru. The four stages include:

- *The Student Stage:* The beginner level, at which one first studies the Veda.

- *The Householder Stage:* The stage at which a person marries and begins a family.

- *The Forest Dweller Stage:* If a man chooses to enter this stage, he leaves his family and property to live amongst nature with a guru who helps him to abandon the distractions of the world and focus on meditation.

- *The Ascetic Stage:* The final stage is when a Hindu practices yoga on his own. Sometimes this stage also includes self-torture as a means to achieving supreme focus and concentration.

Should Christians Practice Yoga?

According to *Yoga Magazine,* 7.5 percent of Americans practice yoga (or 16.5 million people). Of those practicing, the fastest-growing segment is the 18-to-24 age group, which has increased by 46 percent in just one year. Of those not currently practicing yoga, about 25 million said they intended to try yoga within the next 12 months.

It's estimated that Americans spend $2.95 billion a year on yoga classes and products, including equipment, clothing, vacations and media, such as DVDs, videos, books and magazines.[11] There is now even a *Yoga for Christians* book available.[12]

Yet Michael Gleghorn of Probe Ministries, in a well-researched article on yoga, says this:

> Yoga is an ancient spiritual discipline whose central doctrines are utterly incompatible with those of Christianity. Even *hatha yoga,* often considered to be exclusively concerned with physical development, is best understood as merely a means of helping the yogi reach the goal of *samadhi,* or union with "God." Furthermore, we've seen that all yoga, including *hatha,* has the potential to be physically, mentally, and spiritually harmful.[13]

In Hinduism, yoga is the path of human union with the divine Brahman.

In other words, if you're a Christian, the advice is to take up another form of exercise that does not pose concerns to your spiritual beliefs. True yoga has one specific goal: to unite the person to Brahman through experiences of mystical consciousness. Yoga authority Gopi Krishna observes, "All the systems of yoga...are designed to bring about those psychosomatic [mental and physical] changes in the body which are essential for the metamorphosis [change] of consciousness."[14] You may say you don't believe in it, but that's its background.

3. The Way of Devotion

The third way of Hindu salvation is the way of devotion, known as *bhakti yoga*. This is the most popular way among the common people of India. It satisfies the desire for a more emotional and personal approach to religion. This devotion involves a person surrendering to one of the many personal gods and goddesses of Hinduism. This lifetime commitment is expressed through acts of worship, temple rituals, and pilgrimages. Some Hindus conceive of ultimate salvation as absorption into the one divine reality, with all loss of individual existence. Others consider it as heavenly existence in adoration of the personal god.

Hinduism Compared with Biblical Christianity

As we compare the beliefs of Hinduism with the beliefs of biblical Christianity, we observe some striking differences:

Belief	Hindu Perspective	Biblical Perspective
God	There are over 330 million gods.	One God in three persons—Father, Son, and Holy Spirit.
Holy Book	The Vedas, the Upanishads, the Ramayana, the Mahabharata, and the Bhagavad Gita are considered their holy writings. The Bhagavad Gita is considered the most popular and sacred book.	Only the 66 books of the Holy Bible are the authoritative works of Christianity.
Sin	There is no concept of personal sin against a holy God.	All people have sinned against God (except Jesus).
Jesus Christ	Jesus is not seen as the Messiah, God's Son. He did not rise from the dead; he was simply a man who realized his divine nature.	God's perfect son, holy, resurrected, divine (second person of the Trinity), yet also fully human.

Salvation	*Moksha* (freedom from infinite being and selfhood and final self-realization of the truth) is the goal of existence, not salvation.	Obtained only by God's grace through faith in Jesus Christ, not by human effort.
Afterlife	Repeated reincarnation until a person is reabsorbed into Brahman.	At death, all people will enter heaven or hell based on whether they have salvation in Jesus Christ. The Bible does not support the concept of reincarnation.

In the foundational areas of Christian belief, Hinduism does not hold a single similarity with biblical Christianity. Hinduism is not just another way to God; it is a completely opposing system of belief that promotes the worship of a multitude of gods.

Why is Hinduism a big deal? First, those who follow Christ must be aware that Hindu practices are incompatible with Christian living. Careful evaluation should be given to yoga (or other lesser-known exercise programs), literature, film, video games, and other media that promote Hindu religious beliefs.

Second, Christians must be aware of the vast differences between Hinduism and Christianity in order to more effectively live out and communicate Christian beliefs to Hindu followers. One way to approach a follower of Hindu is to simply ask how Hinduism came up with the belief that there are so many gods. This could be followed by sharing the Christian view that there is only one God who created all things. Also, regarding the afterlife, how does a Hindu know he or she will be reincarnated? On what basis is this belief held? Christians believe in a loving God who can be known and experienced—a God who has provided a way to spend eternity with him in heaven for those who put their trust in his son Jesus Christ. Providing caring answers to those whose beliefs are built around a world that is only an illusion of reality can help make a difference to those who are sincerely seeking truth.

Now That You Know

As we have seen, Hinduism is completely different from Christianity at every level. While it is respected as a peaceful religion and is shared by millions worldwide, we who are Christians have an obligation not only to understand Hindus but to assist them in discovering the personal and knowable Jesus of biblical Christianity.

What's with the Enlightenment Thing?

10

uddhism is the world's fourth largest religion, and it continues to have a growing impact worldwide. From films such as *Seven Years in Tibet* to the bestselling *The Zen of Motorcycle Maintenance* and to the popularity of Zen tea in America's coffee shops, Buddhist terms and stories have gone mainstream in today's society.

- 376 million people consider themselves Buddhist.[1]
- Buddhism is the main religion in Hawaii.[2]
- Between three to four million Buddhists live in the United States, the most of any Western nation.[3]
- Buddhism's adherents have included celebrities such as Tina Turner, Phil Jackson (coach of the Los Angeles Lakers), Richard Gere, and Steven Seagal.[4]
- The Dalai Lama has become a prominent spiritual figure for many throughout the world and was the winner of the 1989 Nobel Peace Prize.

Yet even with Buddhism's rise in popularity, most people in our culture have little understanding of its history, beliefs, or practices. In our conversation together in this chapter, we'll zoom through 2600 years of history to discover the origins and thinking of the religion known as Buddhism.

About Buddha

Buddhism begins with Buddha. Buddha, originally known as Siddhartha Gautama, was born in the sixth century B.C. to parents who ruled a small kingdom in modern-day Nepal. A brief look at his life reveals some insightful perspectives for our conversation on this influential faith.

A Sketchy History?

"Buddhism began as an offspring of Hinduism in the country of India. The founder was Siddhartha Gautama. It is not easy to give an accurate historical account of the life of Gautama since *no biography was recorded until five hundred years after his death*. Today, much of his life story is clouded in myths and legends which arose after his death. Even the best historians of our day have several different—and even contradictory—accounts of Gautama's life."

—PATRICK ZUKERAN[5]

His Early Years

From the start, Gautama was considered a special child. On the night of his conception, his mother had a vision of a white elephant. According to tradition, this is the sign of an exceptional child. An astrologer also predicted before Gautama's birth that he would become either a great world leader, or if he experienced much suffering, would become an important spiritual leader.

Gautama's father sought to protect him from suffering to the point that the child grew up behind palace walls without seeing the world around him. Though he married a woman from a different land, their entire relationship developed within the palace walls of his youth. His lifestyle provided for his every need except for the satisfaction of his curiosity.

At age 29, Gautama had his chariot driver take him to the surrounding village area. There, for the first time, he saw what he would later describe as the Four Signs: an old man, a sick man, a corpse in preparation for cremation, and a traveling holy man. With his new-found knowledge, Gautama felt compelled to flee the extravagance of his palace life.

The Great Renunciation

Gautama greatly struggled with the stark contrast between his pampered life and the painful existence endured by many in his community. After a brief time, Gautama left his family, shaved his head, and began a homeless life in nature, now known in Buddhism as the Great Renunciation. While wandering, he met two holy men who taught him the art of meditation. In his pursuits, Gautama began an extended fast to obtain enlightenment.

Despite his human self-determination, he could not reach the level of spirituality he desired. After six long years of seeking, he decided to meditate in one spot. He chose to meditate under a lone Bodhi tree until he found what he desired.

The Awakening

According to Buddhist legends and tradition, one night while sleeping in the crossed-legged lotus position, Gautama fought an inner battle with Mara (the personification of death and evil). By morning, Mara had been defeated, and Gautama awoke with a new sense of clarity. In what is now known as his awakening, Gautama realized that the middle ground between self-denial and self-indulgence provided the best spiritual path for fulfillment.

As Gautama began to share his message, he communicated his way of the middle through what he called the Four Noble Truths. It was said that those who listened to him sensed a special authority to his message and labeled him the *Buddha,* a word that meant "the enlightened one." He continued to spread this message the remainder of his life, traveling throughout his land until the age of 80. He died in peace, believing he was about to enter nirvana.

The Ten Largest National Buddhist Populations

Country	Number of Buddhists
China	102,000,000
Japan	89,650,000
Thailand	55,480,000
Vietnam	49,690,000
Myanmar	41,610,000
Sri Lanka	12,540,000
South Korea	10,920,000
Taiwan	9,150,000
Cambodia	9,130,000
India	7,000,000

Source: Russell Ash, *The Top 10 of Everything* (New York: DK Publishing, 1997), pp. 160-61

The Four Noble Truths

Since Buddhism is built upon the Four Noble Truths, it's important to take a moment to find out what they are. According to tradition, these truths are built upon Buddha's first experience outside the palace walls within which he grew up. However, the teaching of these truths did not begin until years after his awakening.

1. Life Is All About Suffering

Buddha first acknowledged that life is difficult and full of suffering. In addition, reincarnation offers no escape from this struggle. Upon death, birth begins another life, offering more pain. This reoccurring pain leads to a desire to understand its source and find an escape.

2. The Cause of Suffering Is Our Desire and Greed

According to Buddha, the cause of human suffering is greed. At life's core, there are three major evils: hatred, desire, and ignorance. Desire and greed lead to hatred and ignorance of true reality. Selfish desires are seen as the root of all pain and suffering.

3. There Is a Way to Overcome Our Desire and Greed

In Buddhism, there is hope to overcome our human tendency toward greed and selfishness. This hope is built upon the belief that a person can achieve nirvana and escape the endless cycle of suffering.

4. The Path to Happiness and Relief of Suffering Is the Eightfold Path

To achieve nirvana and escape suffering, a person must follow the Eightfold Path. In other words, these four truths are a foundation, but not an end. There are certain steps that must be followed on this middle way before a person can transcend suffering and reach nirvana.

The Eightfold Path

While it is easy to get the idea that knowledge of the Four Noble Truths is enough to get by in Buddhism, the real work begins with the Eightfold Path. The Eightfold Path describes the way to the end of suffering, according to Siddhartha Gautama. Buddhist thinkers say this about the Eightfold Path:

> [It] is a practical guideline to ethical and mental development with the goal of freeing the individual from attachments and delusions; and it finally leads to understanding the truth about all things. *Together with the Four Noble Truths it constitutes the gist of Buddhism.* Great emphasis is put on the practical aspect, because it is only through practice that one can attain a higher level of existence and finally reach Nirvana [which is the blowing out of the flame of desire]. The eight aspects of the path are

not to be understood as a sequence of single steps, instead
they are highly interdependent principles that have to be
seen in relationship with each other.[6]

In their words, these eight aspects are interdependent values that
help people reach higher levels of growth until they reach nirvana.
Nirvana is "not a place, but a total reorientation or state of being
realized as a consequence of the extinction of blinding and binding
attachment."[7] These eight are also often divided into three larger
groupings labeled wisdom, ethical conduct, and mental development.

1. Right Views[8]

Right views are considered the beginning and the end of the
path. It means to see and understand things as they really are and
to realize the Four Noble Truths. It is considered a mental aspect of
wisdom. It means to see things through, to grasp the impermanent
and imperfect nature of worldly objects and ideas, and to understand
the law of karma.

However, right views are not just an intellectual ability. Rather,
right views are reached and improved through all capacities of the
mind. It begins with the insight that all beings are subject to suffering and ends with a complete understanding of the true nature of
all things. Since our view of the world forms our thoughts and our
actions, right views result in right thoughts and right actions.

2. Right Intention

While right views refer to a mental aspect of wisdom, right intention refers to the renunciation of all the pleasures of the senses, a
mental energy that controls our actions. Right intention can be
described as a commitment to ethical and mental self-improvement.
Buddha distinguished three types of right intentions: the intention
of renunciation, which means resistance to desire; the intention of
good will, meaning resistance to feelings of anger; and the intention of
harmlessness, meaning not to think or act violently or aggressively.

3. Right Speech

Right speech is the first principle of ethical practice which teaches one is not to lie, slander, or abuse anyone by idle talk. This is viewed as a guideline to moral discipline. Words can break or save lives, make enemies or friends, start wars or create peace. Buddha said there are four aspects to right speech: abstaining from false speech, especially deliberate lies and deceitful words; abstaining from slanderous speech; abstaining from harsh words that offend or hurt others; and abstaining from meaningless talk that lacks purpose or depth. From a positive angle, we are to tell the truth, speak graciously, and to talk only when necessary.

4. Right Action or Behavior

This second ethical principle involves the body as a natural means of expression and refers to good deeds. Again, the principle is explained in terms of abstinence. There are three aspects to right action: abstaining from harming or killing others, including suicide; abstaining from dishonesty and theft; and abstaining from sexual immorality.

5. Right Livelihood

Right livelihood means that one should earn his or her own living in a positive way and that wealth should be gained legally and peacefully. The Buddha mentions four types of harm that should be avoided: weapons, dealing in living beings (including raising animals for slaughter, the slave trade, and prostitution), working in meat production and butchery, and dealing in alcohol and drugs. Also, any work that would violate the principles of right speech and right action should be avoided.

6. Right Effort

Without effort, which is in itself an act of will, nothing can be achieved. Right effort is detailed in four types of activities that rank in ascending order of perfection: to prevent the arising of unarisen unwholesome states, to abandon unwholesome states that have already arisen, to arouse wholesome states that have not yet arisen, and to maintain and perfect wholesome states already arisen. In other words, right effort includes stopping injustice and promoting justice via one's actions.

7. Right Mindfulness

Right mindfulness is controlled thinking—to be alert, free of desire, and observant. It is the mental ability to see things as they are with clear consciousness. Buddha accounted for this as the Four Foundations of Mindfulness: contemplation of the body, contemplation of feeling (repulsive, attractive, or neutral), contemplation of the state of mind, and contemplation of the phenomena (supernatural/spiritual).[9]

8. Right Meditation or Concentration

Right meditation refers to the development of concentration, the focus of the mind. The Buddhist method of right concentration is achieved through the practice of meditation. After abandoning all sensuous pleasures, all evil qualities, and all joy and sorrow, then the meditating mind can focus on the four degrees of meditation, which are produced by concentration. Through this practice it eventually becomes natural to apply elevated levels of concentration in everyday situations.

Other Distinctives of Buddhism

Here are seven additional major elements of Buddhism:

Meditation

As indicated in the eighth portion of the Eightfold Path, meditation is a central focus in Buddhism. It is through meditation that one understands reality and truth. Meditation takes particular priority in Zen Buddhism.

Nirvana

Buddhists believe in reincarnation and teach that the only escape from an endless cycle of rebirths is to achieve higher levels of growth that eventually reach nirvana, a state of passionless peace. Donald K. Swearer describes the concept of nirvana:

> Nirvana has been a troublesome idea for students of Buddhism. Just what is it? The term itself does not offer much help. LIKE NOT-SELF (an-atta), nirvana is a negative term. Literally, it means the "blowing out" of the flame of desire, the negation of suffering (Dukkha). This implies that nirvana is not to be thought of as a place but as a total reorientation or state of being realized as a consequence of the extinction of blinding and binding attachment. Thus, at least, nirvana implies that the kind of existence one has achieved is inconceivable in the ordinary terms of the world.[10]

Buddha never gave an exact definition of nirvana, but it can be described in this way:

> There is disciples, a condition, where there is neither earth nor water, neither air nor light, neither limitless space, nor limitless time, neither any kind of being, neither ideation nor non-ideation, neither this world nor that world. There is neither arising nor passing-away, nor dying, neither cause nor effect, neither change nor standstill.[11]

According to Buddhism, the unity of the human personality is an illusion. The reality is a constantly changing arrangement of the different elements that make up the world. Belief in the self is rejected. *I* and *my* are concepts bearing no relation to truth. So nirvana is sometimes mistakenly described as nothingness.

The Tripitaka, an early Buddhist scripture, defines nirvana as follows:

> The area where there is no earth, water, fire and air; it is not the region of infinite space, nor that of infinite consciousness; it is not the region of nothing at all, nor the border between distinguishing and not distinguishing; not

this world nor the other world; where there is neither sun nor moon. I will not call it coming and going, nor standing still, nor fading away nor beginning. It is without foundation, without continuation, and without stopping. It is the end of suffering.[12]

Notice that nirvana is defined only by negatives. This is quite different from the place Jesus described as heaven. There, believers in Jesus Christ will have a new body (Philippians 3:21), and there will be no sin (Revelation 22:3) or death (Revelation 21:4). Those who go to heaven will enjoy fellowship with God, loved ones, and friends who put their belief in Christ. The Bible's message ends with a longing for heaven, with the apostle John urging, "Come, Lord Jesus" (Revelation 22:20).

Samsara

Samsara is the belief that each life is simply a flow of being that consists of suffering, change, and reincarnation. Buddhists don't consider their personalities to be permanent, because they are shared over many lifetimes in multiple forms.

Renunciation

This is the belief that the only way to achieve real meaning in life is to "let go" or renounce life as we percieve it to be. Humans grasp for a life that does not exist. Therefore, we must renounce this grasping in order to reach true understanding.

Reincarnation

What you or I might consider to be a "person" is only part of a chain of life. People are reborn into one of several realms based on their progress in this life. As a result, the mental state of a person at the point of death (the extent to which they have renounced all desires) is of vital importance to the Buddhist.

Reincarnated Buddhas

Gautama was the first Buddha, but not the only one. As practicing

Buddhists reach enlightenment, they can become Buddhas ("enlightened ones") as well. This is the ultimate goal of each Buddhist—to become enlightened and reach nirvana.

The Three Jewels

While Buddhism lacks strict theological beliefs in many areas, the concept of the three jewels is a central teaching in nearly all forms of Buddhism. It consists of Buddha, dharma (true understanding), and sangha, a community of monks who live out and promote true understanding to others.

What Is Zen?

Zen Buddhism isn't the most popular form of Buddhism in America, but it sure receives the most hype in bookstores and popular films. Zen is a form of Buddhism that places great importance on moment-by-moment awareness and seeing deeply into the nature of things by direct experience. In this sense it is similar to Kabbalah or mysticism because it focuses on ongoing mystical and personal revelation. The word *Zen* roughly translates as "meditation."

But is Zen a religion? According to one of its key writings:

> Is Zen a religion? It is not a religion in the sense that the term is popularly understood; for Zen has no God to worship, no ceremonial rites to observe, no future abode to which the dead are destined, and, last of all, Zen has no soul whose welfare is to be looked after by somebody else and whose immortality is a matter of intense concern with some people.[13]

As a result, Zen rejects traditional teaching and focuses on personal experience. Historically, it grew in popularity throughout China and has also been associated with Taoist philosophy. Its American popularity rests mostly on its personalized focus and how it has been embraced by certain celebrity personalities.

Buddhism and Christianity

Here are the three major differences found between Buddhism and Christianity:

1. *In Buddhism a person works out his salvation by following certain steps; in Christianity a person receives salvation as a gift resulting in following Christ.* While human efforts are important in all religions, Christianity's focus on a relationship provided by Jesus is uniquely different from Buddhist teachings.

2. *In Buddhism a person is motivated to escape suffering; in Christianity a person is motivated by love for God and others.* There's a big difference between escaping pain and showing love. In Buddhism, love is just another element among others. But in Christianity, followers love God first, then people (Matthew 22:34-40).

3. *In Buddhism a person is focused primarily on individual enlightenment; in Christianity a person is focused primarily on serving God and others.* Christianity has often fallen into more individualized forms, but has historically focused on service to God first and then to others. Even Jesus, Christianity's founder, said that in obedience to the Father, he came *to serve* others rather than to be served.[14]

The most fundamental difference lies in the difference between the person of Jesus and the person of Buddha. As apologist Patrick Zukeran well explains, "After a comparative study, I came to realize Buddha was a great teacher who lived a noble life, but Christ is the unique revelation of God who is to be worshipped as our eternal Lord and Savior."[15] Here is a comparison chart:

Belief	Buddhist Perspective	Biblical Perspective
God	Denies the existence of a personal God.	One God in three persons— Father, Son, and Holy Spirit.
Holy Book	The Four Noble Truths and the Eightfold Path.	The 66 books of the Holy Bible are the authoritative works of Christianity.

Sin	There is no concept of personal sin against a holy God.	All people have sinned (except Jesus).
Jesus Christ	A wise sage (perhaps enlightened), whose teachings were distorted by Christian myths.	God's perfect son, holy, resurrected, divine (second person of the Trinity), yet also fully human.
Salvation	Through following the right steps, a person may eventually escape the endless series of reincarnations and achieve nirvana.	Obtained only by God's grace through faith in Jesus Christ, not by human effort.
Afterlife	Repeated reincarnation until a person reaches nirvana.	At death, all people will enter heaven or hell based on whether they have salvation in Jesus Christ. The Bible does not teach reincarnation, annihilation (ending of the soul), or the existence of purgatory.

As Josh McDowell, author of *Handbook of Today's Religions*, has noted:

> There are radical differences between Buddhism and Christianity that make any attempt of reconciliation between the two faiths impossible. The Buddhistic world view is basically monistic. That is, the existence of a personal creator and Lord is denied. The world operates by natural power and law, not divine command.[16]

We've discussed the two largest Eastern religions, yet have not touched on other Eastern religions followed by tens of millions of additional people. In our next chapter, we'll continue our conversation by looking at three other highly influential Eastern religions that impact our world today. Along the way we'll see that Hinduism and Buddhism have influenced these religions, yet each one includes a new emphasis that has had an effect on many peoples and cultures.

What's with All the -isms?

11

onfucianism, Taoism, and Shintoism are all influential Eastern religions. Though they do not have the large numbers of followers found in Hinduism and Buddhism, they still have a significant impact worldwide:

- Over six million people practice Confucianism, including 26,000 in North America.

- Taoism has about 20 million followers, mostly in Taiwan, with roughly 30,000 in North America.

- Shintoism is the largest religion in Japan and was once its state religion. Some sources indicate approximately three to four million followers, though other studies have shown that at least 40 percent of Japanese adults are adherents of Shintoism. Statistics vary greatly in part because Shintoism is often practiced in combination with Buddhism or other Eastern religions.

- Combined, nearly 30 million people follow one of these three religions, mostly in Asia. This would make them the world's ninth largest faith, with more adherents than Judaism.[1]

One key reason to study these three faiths together is because of their similar positions on ethics. Unlike most of the religions we have reviewed to this point, they focus very little on God, but rather prefer to focus on the personal responsibility to live a moral life. As such, some have categorized these faiths as philosophies rather than religions. But, as we will see, each definitely includes aspects of both.

Confucianism: More than Confusion

Confucianism is built upon the traditions of Confucius, a man whose real name was K'ung Fu Tzu. He was born about 550 B.C., the youngest of 11 children in an upper-class family, in the principality of Lu, which is located in present-day Shantung. He was a contemporary of the Buddha (although they probably never met) and lived immediately before Socrates and Plato.

Confucius was a moral and upright man who lived in a culture that was neither. He believed that resistance to change was futile, but that nobility should not be abandoned. As a result, he considered it his purpose to live out the idea of the noble life. He invested most of his adult years traveling to advise the common people as well as civic leaders on ethical standards of leadership.

Specifically, Confucius believed that culture as a whole was a reflection of the character of the ruling class. The way of the leaders influenced the way of the followers. If leaders were good, then the people who followed would be good. If leaders were selfish or cruel, then the people would act likewise. Though this message did not gain popularity at the time, his words gained strength with the passage of time and helped transform Chinese society.

Despite the Chinese Communist government's attempts to remove the spread of Confucianism, its principles continue to find followers among many Chinese people. Even among China's leaders the influence of Confucius remains. As Marcus Bach has written:

> One thing that the Communist regime will never be able
> to do is to get Confucius out of China. Some say it has not
> been tried. Others contend there is no use trying. China's...
> people know Confucius as well as America's millions know

about Christ. We do not have a state religion, but we are predominantly Christian. China does not have a state religion, but it is predominantly Confucian.[2]

The Spread of Confucianism

The spread of Confucianism after the death of Confucius arose in large part due to his extensive writings. Several hundred years after he died, two particular schools of thought emerged within Confucianism that form the two major branches of Confucianism today:

- *Mencius (371–289 B.C.):* His belief was that humans are basically good and that intuition can help a person to determine the appropriateness of certain actions. He taught that the seeds of goodness existed within everyone, but they must be nurtured to develop well. As a result, Mencius and his adherents were early advocates of governmental democracy and believed the majority's thoughts would be best for a society's leadership.

- *Xunzi (300–230 B.C.):* He believed that humans are innately evil. His focus was upon training that helped individuals overcome the evil nature within. As a result, Xunzi emphasized rules and codes of conduct that could help people to change.

As you might expect, the teachings of Mencius were more popular and continue to remain so today. Different forms of Confucianism have continued to develop throughout the generations as the faith spread to neighboring countries and cultures, but the core beliefs are still the same. Many Westerners who visit China say the philosophy of civilized behavior still prevails today.

The Beliefs of Confucianism

Confucianism is not about man relating to God. Rather, it is an ethical system that teaches people how to interact with one another.

While Confucianism lacks a creedal system as found in many religions, it holds strong beliefs regarding two important areas of life: the value of relationships, and key values within those relationships.

- *The Five Relationships:* Confucius taught that the most important relationships in life are...

  1. the parent-child relationship
  2. the ruler-subject relationship
  3. the husband-wife relationship
  4. the relationships between siblings
  5. the relationships between friends

- *The Six Key Relationship Values:* Having a relationship is not enough. Confucius taught that these relationships must be developed through...

  1. *li*—proper conduct
  2. *hsiao*—love between family members
  3. *yi*—righteousness, decency, and virtue
  4. *xin*—honesty and trust
  5. *jen*—kindness
  6. *chung*—loyalty and faithfulness

Because Confucianism has ties to other Eastern religions, beliefs regarding the afterlife, sin, and other areas are often determined by the beliefs in other Eastern religions.

The Writings of Confucianism

Confucianism's core teachings are recorded in nine key books. Each was written individually, then the books were compiled, in the twelfth century, into two sets:

- *The Five Classics:* These books are said to have been written before the time of Confucius, though their dating is often disputed:

1. *Shi Jing:* a collection of 300 songs and poems

2. *Shu Jing:* a collection of historical documents attributed to the early rulers of China

3. *Li Ji:* writings regarding rituals

4. *Chun Qui:* an ancient account of Lu, the home region of Confucius

5. *I Ching:* Sixty-four hexagrams—symbols of broken and continuous lines—with special meanings. This is the most popular book of the collection.[3]

- *The Four Books:* These books include the writings of Confucius and Mencius:

  1. *Lun Yu:* also called the Analects, it is a record of the sayings of Confucius[4]

  2. *Chung Yung:* the "doctrine of the mean," which includes a wide variety of teachings[5]

  3. *Ta Hsueh:* also called the Book of Great Learning

  4. *Meng Tzu:* the writings of Mencius

Together, these books form the basis for all of Confucianism and remain popular today.

So how should we view Confucianism? Josh McDowell and Don Stewart, in their book *Handbook of Today's Religions,* wrote:

> The ethical system taught by Confucius has much to commend it, for virtue is something to desire highly. However, the ethical philosophy Confucius espoused was one of self-effort, leaving no room or need for God. Confucius taught that man can do it all by himself if he only follows the way of the ancients, while Christianity teaches that man does not have the capacity to save himself but is in desperate need of a savior. Confucius also hinted that human nature was basically good. This thought was developed by later Confucian teachers and became a cardinal belief of Confucianism. The Bible, on the other hand,

teaches that man is basically sinful and left to himself is completely incapable of performing ultimate good.[6]

Despite the many positive traits in Confucianism, it is ultimately inadequate and incompatible with Christianity, as seen in the chart below:

Belief	Confucian Perspective	Biblical Perspective
God	Denies the existence of a personal God.	One God in three persons—Father, Son, and Holy Spirit.
Holy Book	The Five Classics and the Four Books.	Only the 66 books of the Holy Bible are the authoritative works of Christianity.
Sin	Humans are basically good rather than sinful.	All people have sinned (except Jesus).
Jesus Christ	Does not speak definitively regarding Jesus, yet disregards the supernatural and would reject the physical resurrection of Jesus.	God's perfect son, holy, resurrected, divine (second person of the Trinity), yet also fully human.
Salvation	Salvation is a human process dependent upon one's own efforts.	Obtained only by God's grace through faith in Jesus Christ, not by human effort.
Afterlife	There is no definitive teaching regarding the afterlife. The emphasis is on proper living during this life.	At death, all people will enter heaven or hell based on whether they have salvation in Jesus Christ.

As Sir Norman Anderson has stated, "So the contrast between [Confucius'] teaching and that of the apostolic proclamation of forgiveness, new life, and eternal salvation through a historical person (to whose life, atoning death, resurrection, and ascension they could actually testify) is obvious."[7]

Taoism: The Way of Nature

Taoism is closely related to Confucianism. Both developed in the same region and have often shared some of the same followers. The major difference is that instead of focusing on ethical living, Taoism focuses on nature. In fact, *Tao* means "the way," as in "the way of nature."

What Is Taoism?

Taoists claim that defining their religion is impossible. However, in order to offer some sort of explanation, we can begin by defining *Tao*, which means "the natural order," or "the way the universe works." To follow the Tao, one must yield to inaction and accept what comes his way. The aim is to achieve harmony with all that is by pursuing inaction and effortlessness. Taoism gradually evolved an elaborate mythological system and incorporated notions of spirit possession, alchemy, and divination. True Taoism claims to be a religion of receptivity.

However, this understanding must not be taken to mean it advocates total withdrawal. True inaction in Taoism is defined as the most efficient possible action, the most spontaneous possible action, and the most creative possible action.

Who Started Taoism?

Taoism has its roots in a figure named Lao-Tzu, of whom little is known. Many believe Lao-Tzu was not one person, but rather a team of people. Traditionally, he has been described as a wise man who lived in the same time period as Confucius and passed his teachings along to a border guard for safekeeping. This guard is said to have accurately copied his words into the book we now know as the *Tao Te Ching*, the official book of Taoism.

Another story says that Lao-Tzu was named Plum-Tree-Ears by his mother because he was born under the shadow of a plum tree and his ears were unusually long. However, he was known to the people as Lao-Tzu, meaning "the old philosopher." He supposedly held an important post as curator of the imperial archives at Loyang, the capital city in the state of Ch'u.

His work in a government post became tiresome, for Lao-tzu disapproved of the tyranny of the rulers and the idea of government itself. Lao-tzu came to believe that men were meant to live simply and without honors. Consequently, he resigned his post and returned home.

Because his opinions had gathered unwanted students and disciples, Lao-Tzu left his house to seek privacy from curiosity seekers. He bought a cart and a black ox and set out toward the border of the province, leaving corrupt society behind. However, at the crossing of the border, his friend Yin Hsi, the guard, recognized him and would not allow him to pass.

Yin Hsi exhorted Lao-Tzu, "You have always kept to yourself like a hermit and have never written down your teachings. Yet many know them. Now you wish to leave and retire beyond our borders. I will not let you cross until you have written down the essentials of your teachings."

Lao-Tzu returned after three days with a small treatise entitled *The Tao Te King*, or *The Way and Its Power*. Then he left into the sunset on a water buffalo, never to be heard of again. Whatever the case may be, the little book that was left behind became the basis of a new religion.[8]

Taoism for Your Health

In North America, Taoism is often better known from the techniques of tai chi. An article in *Arthritis Today* says,

Along with other Chinese imports, such as acupuncture and herbs, tai chi is becoming popular in the West. It appeals to people of all ages because it's not intimidating. Seniors particularly like tai chi because the slow, synchronized movements are easy to learn and to perform...Once scarce, classes can now be found through YMCAs, some churches, community centers, karate schools and even through some health maintenance organizations. Tai chi is taught at some summer camps for children with juvenile arthritis. In Australia, a tai chi program designed especially for people with arthritis is supported and taught by the Arthritis Foundation of Australia.[9]

But tai chi is more than just a form of exercise. According to mystic authority Edwina Gately,

> Chi is considered to be an energy that flows through the body. Acupuncture and the practice of tai chi, meditation in motion, are said to allow this energy to achieve a balance between the opposing principles of yin and yang, thus ultimately leading to physical and spiritual wellbeing. This theory is based on the philosophy of Taoism.
>
> Tao is the name given to a force that flows through every living being as well as the universe.[10]

Tai chi is specifically designed for spiritual growth, but a spiritual growth very distinct from that found in Christianity. For Christians, it is important to evaluate and avoid practices in which the intent is to focus energy upon other gods.

Taoism's Sacred Writing: Tao-te Ching

The *Tao-te Ching* is a small book of approximately 5500 words, and it instructs rulers in the art of government. It teaches that less government is better, and that a ruler should lead by nonaction. Historically, Chinese leaders have not taken the book's political teachings seriously. However, there is a philosophical side to the *Tao-te Ching* that has had an enormous impact on the nation. The work teaches individuals how to endure in the midst of terrible calamities, which have been common in China through the ages. It advocates staying in the background, which will help one's odds of survival.

There is an ongoing debate as to when the *Tao-te Ching* was composed. The traditionalist point of view says the work was composed by Lao-Tzu, a contemporary of Confucius, in the sixth century B.C. The basis for this date is the biography of Lao-Tzu in the Shih-chi (Records of the Historian), which dates from about 100 B.C. Others view the work as having been formally compiled about 300 B.C. because of its similarity of style to other works composed in that period. The historical setting, they argue, fits more with this turbulent era.

Next to Lao-Tzu, the most important figure in Taoism is Chuang-Tzu, one of Lau-Tzu's original followers. Chuang-Tzu was a prolific author who lived during the fourth century B.C. and wrote 33 books. He was a clever writer who popularized the teachings of Lao-Tzu.

We can see the Taoist thinking of Chuang-Tzu in the following words:

> Once I, Chuang Chou, dreamed that I was a butterfly and was happy as a butterfly...Suddenly I awoke, and there I was, visibly Chou. I do not know whether it was Chou dreaming that he was a butterfly or the butterfly dreaming it was Chou. Between Chou and the butterfly there must be some distinction. This is called the transformation of things.[11]

Taoism's Beliefs

Taoism teaches that the primary goal in life is to conform to the way of the Tao, or the way of nature. While Taoist philosophy varies greatly on many issues, two primary beliefs are held in common among Taoists:

- *The Principle of Wu Wei (inaction):* How does a person accomplish inaction? The *Tao-te Ching* teaches this can be done by practicing the basic attitude of *wu wei*, which literally means "inaction."

  This principle communicates stopping all aggression by living according to what comes naturally and is spontaneous. People are to live passively, avoiding all stress to better communicate with nature. In doing this, their lives will flow with the Tao.

- *Yin and Yang:* A concept in both Confucianism and Taoism is the belief in the yin and yang. According to their beliefs, though all things emanate from the Tao, there are certain forces that are contrary to each other, such as good and evil and life and death. The negative force is called the *yin* and the positive force the *yang*.

Communicating the Yin and Yang

Yin	Yang
Female	Male
Evil	Good
Darkness	Light
Death	Life
Winter	Summer
Passive	Active
Negative	Positive
Earth	Heaven

The concept of yin and yang is used to explain the fluidity in both people and nature. According to Taoism, "to blend with the cycle (of the universe) without effort is to become one with the Tao and so find fulfillment."[12] Though the Tao may have a temporary appeal, it is ultimately unfulfilling. Taoism leaves a person defenseless and alone in facing the problems of evil, forgiveness, power for living, and the afterlife. The only Taoist solution is to ignore and withdraw from facing reality.

In contrast, Christianity offers a person a personal relationship with the God of the universe, who can remove the problem, give eternal life and forgiveness, and promises to provide peace and his personal presence when we face problems. Here are some additional differences between Taoism and biblical Christianity:

Belief	Taoist Perspective	Biblical Perspective
God	Denies the existence of a personal God. Believes only in an impersonal creative force behind the universe.	One God in three persons— Father, Son, and Holy Spirit.
Holy Book	The Tao-te Ching, a short 5500-word document that serves as the Taoist holy book.	Only the 66 books of the Holy Bible are the authoritative works of Christianity.

Sin	Provides no clear distinction between right and wrong. Inaction is emphasized rather than moral absolutes.	All people have sinned against God (except Jesus).
Jesus Christ	Does not speak definitively regarding Jesus. Taoist beliefs do not provide a need for a Savior such as Jesus, nor do they say that there is any one way to God.	God's perfect son, holy, resurrected, divine (second person of the Trinity), yet also fully human.
Salvation	Salvation is a human process dependent upon one's own efforts.	Obtained only by God's grace through faith in Jesus Christ, not by human effort.
Afterlife	There is no definitive teaching regarding the afterlife, though heaven is mentioned in its writings.	At death, all people will enter heaven or hell based on whether they have salvation in Jesus Christ.

Shintoism: The Way of the Gods

Shinto continues to influence millions of people today, especially in Japan, where it formerly existed as a state religion.

Did You Know...

...there are over 80,000 Shinto shrines in Japan to honor the gods?

What Is Shinto?

The word *Shinto* comes from the Chinese word *shen-tao,* which means "the way of the gods." This touches on the core belief of Shinto, the *kami,* or a belief in numerous spirits who influence the acts of individuals during their daily activities.

In its earliest form, Shinto was without name, text, or creeds. It is one of the world's oldest faiths, with origins reaching to prehistoric times. Today, Shinto retains its focus on the spiritual workings of the natural world around us, whether in farming, fertility, or everyday work-related activities. It is not uncommon for Japanese business leaders to pray to the *kami* for success in sales or for students to ask the *kami* for success on school tests.

The Two Defining Dates of Shinto

In modern history, Shinto has undergone two major periods of dramatic change. Both revolve around key dates, one in the nineteenth century and one in the twentieth.

- *1868—The Meiji Restoration:* Throughout the ages, Shinto has blended, as a religion, with other Eastern religions, especially Buddhism. During the 1700s, Shinto followers began a renewal effort to distinguish their teachings and practices from those of other faiths. In 1868, the Meiji Restoration officially separated Shinto from Buddhist practices, becoming a driving factor behind Japanese nationalism.

- *1945—Post World War II:* After World War II, Shinto was no longer the state religion of Japan. Public funds could no longer be used for shrines, and Emperor Hirohito renounced his claim to be divine. Though Shinto remains highly popular in Japan today, its influence within official government practices has taken on a different look.

The Two Sides of Shinto:

It is important to note that Shinto exists in two different forms:

1. *Popular Shinto:* Shinto shrines exist in nearly every neighborhood in Japan, and Shinto strongly influences thinking on the popular cultural level.

2. *Political Shinto:* Before 1945, Shinto was integrated into politics. Since then, the two have remained separated.[13]

Basic Shinto Practices and Beliefs

Shinto is high on ritual and low on beliefs. Followers of Shinto utilize four affirmations that serve as essential values in their faith today:

- *The affirmation of family and tradition:* Shinto reveres the major life events, especially birth and marriage.

- *The affirmation of reverence toward nature:* Closeness to nature is a central component of Shinto devotion.

- *The affirmation of physical cleanliness:* This includes both ritual cleanliness and physical cleanliness. It's not the cliché "cleanliness is next to godliness," but "cleanliness *is* godliness."

- *The affirmation of* matsuri: *Matsuri* are festivals held in honor of one or more *kami* (spirits).

The "Non-religious" Aspects of Shinto

Unlike many religions, Shinto lacks a founder, a sacred set of writings, and a set form of worship, creeds, or formal religious laws.

In addition to these four affirmations, Shinto holds four additional beliefs distinct to its faith:

- *The Sun Goddess:* The sun goddess is the only deity recognized in Shinto. This is the deity Amaterasu, from whom the imperial family of Japan traces its roots. This imperial family, once considered divine, remains in high esteem today.

- *The* Kami: *Kami* are spirits that can take the form of wind, rain, mountains, rivers, or even fertility. According to Shinto tradition, over eight million of these spirits exist. They have power to help those who ask them for help. Shinto claims humans become *kami* after they have died.

- *The Goodness of Humanity:* In Shinto, people are considered basically good. As a result, there is no belief in the Judeo-Christian concept of original sin or sinful acts and thoughts before a holy God.

- *Multiple Religions:* In Shinto, it is permissible to practice Shinto alongside another religion or philosophy. Many Japanese follow both Shinto and Buddhism in varying degrees.[14]

It's a Little-known Fact

Did you know that the paper-folding art of origami originated within the Shinto religion? *Origami* literally means "paper of the spirits," and these artistic creations are commonly used to decorate Shinto temples.

Though Shinto is no longer the state religion in Japan, its influence is still very evident upon popular culture. For example, before sumo wrestling bouts, many Shinto-inspired ceremonies must be performed, such as purifying the wrestling arena by sprinkling it with salt. The Japanese emphasis on proper greetings and respectful phrasings originates from the ancient Shinto belief in *kotodama* (words with a magical effect on the world). Many Japanese cultural customs, such as using wooden chopsticks and removing one's shoes before entering a building, also have their origin in Shinto beliefs and practices.[15]

While Shinto displays some culturally positive aspects, its spiritual beliefs are contrary to those of biblical Christianity. A belief in the basic goodness of all people, prayers to spirits, and acknowledgment of multiple gods are all concepts that contradict the teachings of Jesus and the Bible. More differences are evident below:

Belief	Shinto's Perspective	Biblical Perspective
God	Believes in a multitude of gods, the chief being the sun goddess Amaterasu.	One God in three persons—Father, Son, and Holy Spirit.

Holy Book	The Ko-ji-ki ("records of ancient matters") and Nihon-gi (the "chronicles of Japan") are the most influential writings in Shinto.	Only the 66 books of the Holy Bible are the authoritative works of Christianity.
Sin	Teaches the basic goodness and superiority of its people rather than clear distinctions between right and wrong.	All people have sinned against God (except Jesus).
Jesus Christ	Jesus is not seen as a Savior because there is no perceived need for salvation.	God's perfect son, holy, resurrected, divine (second person of the Trinity), yet also fully human.
Salvation	Salvation is unnecessary because those who follow Shinto consider themselves basically good.	Obtained only by God's grace through faith in Jesus Christ, not by human effort.
Afterlife	There is no definitive teaching regarding the afterlife, though heaven is mentioned in Shinto writings.	At death, all people will enter heaven or hell based on whether they have salvation in Jesus Christ.

Let's be clear. Comparing religions is educational, but it is also important personally. Not all religions are the same. They certainly don't teach the same things about God, people, creation, Jesus, salvation, or the afterlife. What we hope you realize is that Christianity claims it is the one religion God gave to humanity. This claim is backed up by the facts the God of Christianity revealed hundreds of years in advance—the facts that would surround Jesus' perfect life, death, and resurrection from the grave.

All these supernatural prophecies (predictions) have been fulfilled. Christianity also claims it can meet your personal needs better than any other religion, and empower you where you have failed in your own strength. Finally, eternity is coming. Was Jesus right about heaven and hell? We will all die and find out. But once we die, our destination is irreversible. The time to investigate and decide is now.

This chapter completes our review of the major Eastern religions, and now we'll continue our conversation by turning to the major multigod and anti-God religions—the New Age movement, agnosticism, and atheism.

Part Five | # Multigod and Anti-God Religions

p to now we've looked at the world's largest one-God religions, alternative religions, and Eastern religions. In the final section of this book, we will consider the impact of three of the most influential religious movements that don't fit any of the above categories, yet impact millions of people in our world today.

For instance, according to Adherents.com, the category "secular/nonreligious/agnostic/atheist" includes 1.1 billion people. Throw in spiritism/New Age, and we have another 115 million followers. While these categories are nontraditional, they are certainly influential, with large numbers of adherents.[1]

First we'll look at the New Age movement. This primarily American movement combines Eastern religions and spiritism in a way that is so popular that it has gained its own shelf space in today's bookstores and is practiced among some of today's top celebrities.

Then we'll consider the enormous impact of agnosticism and atheism in our culture. With a new surge of popularity spurred by bestselling books such as *god Is Not Great, The God Delusion, Letter to a Christian Nation,* and *Breaking the Spell: Religion as Natural Phenomenon,* the question of whether God is there at all has once again attracted considerable attention.

In my 27 years of television interviews with some of the most authoritative figures in world religions, I (John) have noticed that nearly one out of every three programs I've produced has touched upon some aspect of the New Age, spiritism, or agnosticism and atheism. Consequently there's no question these religions and movements are of tremendous importance to many people all around us. For that reason we invite you to learn what these adherents believe.

What's So New About New Age?

12

"Recent surveys of US adults indicate that around 20% of Americans hold at least some New Age beliefs."

—GEORGE BARNA[1]

"As many as 12 million Americans are active New Age participants. Another 30 million are 'avidly interested.'"

—FROM *WORLD RELIGIONS & CULTS 101*[2]

"36% of Americans believe that astrology is scientific, and 25% now believe in reincarnation."

—RUSSELL CHANDLER, *UNDERSTANDING THE NEW AGE*[3]

World-famous psychiatrist Dr. Elisabeth Kubler-Ross, who authored the widely read book *On Death and Dying*, and Dr. Norman Shealy, who was a prestigious neurosurgeon who taught at Harvard University, both had mystical experiences that led them to become involved in New Age beliefs and practices. I (John) invited both to be guests on my television program.

Dr. Elisabeth Kubler-Ross told our audience that for most of her life she was an agnostic. But after leaving Zurich, Switzerland to teach at the University of Chicago, she allegedly had an out-of-body experience one night, during which she met spirit guides who gave her a full physical healing. She claimed that from that time onward, she had talked to the dead; lived during the time of Christ as Isabel, one of his teachers; and communicated with materialized spirits called entities. After her New Age initiation she went on to catalog over 20,000 cases of near-death experiences in which people who had stopped breathing and supposedly died entered and passed through a dark tunnel, saw a great light coming toward them and surrounding them with love, entered a very beautiful scenic place, and met loved ones who had died earlier.

The first time I saw Dr. Norman Shealy was on NBC. Jane Pauley visited his office and watched how he treated and diagnosed patients. After examining a patient, he would run the usual scientific tests. Upon determining what was wrong and the course of treatment that was necessary, he would then call clairvoyant Carolyn Myss, who was sitting in an office 1100 miles away in another city. She would then do a psychic scan of the patient sitting in Dr. Shealy's office. Dr. Shealy told Jane Pauley that if Myss's diagnosis did not agree with his, then he would not proceed in treating the patient. After watching this interview on "The New Medicine Today," I contacted Dr. Shealy and invited him to come on my program along with some Christian doctors.

As I prepared for the television interviews, I wanted to know what Dr. Shealy thought Carolyn Myss was doing in her psychic scans. Here's how she described it herself: "Since 1985, I have worked with Norm Shealy using clairvoyant abilities to assist him in identifying the emotional, psychological, and spiritual stress factors within a person's inner world that have contributed to the creation of a physical disease. The data I provide Norm is that which cannot be measured clinically nor determined through blood samples. The process through which we work is simple: Norm calls me at my home in New Hampshire while his patient is in his Springfield, Missouri office. I require only the name and age of a patient and the patient's

permission to do the reading. I then share with Norm the information that I intuitively perceive about that patient's life...In almost
all cases, people's energy fields reveal how they feel about themselves. The combination of these emotional stresses, combined with
the intensity of the stresses, indicates to me what specific physical
dysfunction exists."

Some of the people who are involved in the New Age movement
are among those who normally enjoy the highest degree of public
confidence—physicians, scientists, educators, psychotherapists, and
even clergymen. Yet they violate this public trust by turning to the
dubious realms of Eastern mysticism to provide people with help
and guidance.

Where do the practitioners of holistic health techniques and New
Age beliefs get their information? Can we believe them? What did
Jesus Christ and the Bible say about talking to spirits?

What Is the New Age Movement?

"The New Age movement is the most powerful social force in the world
today."

—DR. CARL RASCHKE, PROFESSOR OF RELIGIOUS STUDIES, UNIVERSITY OF DENVER[4]

The New Age movement refers to a worldview or philosophy of
life that many people hold to. It can be called a religion because it
is based on religious views. For example, New Age adherents hold
to pantheism, a belief that everything is a part of God. That is,
God is all, and all is God. They believe that every person is part of
God, even though those outside of the New Age movement might
not realize it.

Through mystical experiences, or while practicing techniques that
alter one's state of consciousness, people are powerfully persuaded
that the religious worldview of the New Age is true. An example of
this is Shirley MacLaine. During a mystical experience in a hot tub,
here is what she said she was led to believe:

My whole body seemed to float. Slowly, slowly I became the water...I felt the inner connection of my breathing with the pulse of the energy around me. In fact, I was the air, the water, the darkness, the walls, the bubbles, the candle, the wet rocks under the water, and even the sound of the rushing river outside.[5]

On the basis of experiences such as these, New Age followers have concluded that they must be one with the universe and are part of God. This has also led them to believe they have discovered untapped human potential, an alleged divine power that they believe exists in all people. New Age practitioners want to help everybody discover this power and personally realize their oneness with God. They believe that by getting all people to exercise their potential, it will be possible to bring about world unity and peace.

Many New Age adherents profess to having encounters with spirit guides or spirit beings. These spirit beings, allegedly good spirits, claim to be people who have died and who now reside in the spirit world to guide and help others spiritually, or they profess to be extraordinary spiritual entities who exist to help humans.

The Financial Influence of the New Age Movement

According to Marilyn McGuire, executive director of the New Age Publishing and Retailing Alliance, there are some 2500 occult bookstores in the United States and over 3000 publishers of occult books and journals. Sales of New Age books in particular are estimated at $1 billion a year. This makes the New Age movement a multibillion dollar industry, and such industries receive the attention of corporate America and those in power.[6]

A (Very) Brief History of the New Age Movement

According to one source,

New Age teachings became popular during the 1970s as an alternative to what some perceived as the failure of Christianity and the failure of Secular Humanism to provide spiritual and ethical guidance for the future. Its roots are traceable to many sources: Astrology, Channeling, Hinduism, Gnostic traditions, Spiritualism, Taoism, Theosophy, Wicca, and other Neo-pagan traditions. The movement started in England in the 1960s, where many of these elements were well established. Small groups, such as the Findhorn Community in Inverness and the Wrekin Trust, formed. The movement quickly became international. Early New Age mileposts in North America were a *"New Age Seminar"* run by the Association for Research and Enlightenment, and the establishment of the *East-West Journal* in 1971. Actress Shirley MacLaine is perhaps their most famous current figure.[7]

Recent years have shown a renewed interest in New Age practices, though sometimes under different names. For instance, the 2006 bestselling book *The Secret* by Rhonda Byrne promotes many of the practices promoted in New Age writings and seminars.[8]

The Impact of the New Age Movement

How much impact has this movement had on our culture? Perhaps much more than many people realize. The New Age movement has touched almost every major segment of society, including:

Health Care

New Age adherents have been strong proponents of holistic health care, focusing on the whole person and his or her surroundings. They also emphasize *energy,* not matter. They teach that we can unblock and redirect energy flow in the body as a means of healing through methods such as acupuncture, acupressure, therapeutic touch, and biofeedback. For instance, Yale University professor of medicine Bernie Siegel said years ago, "...applied to physical illness, the most widely used and successful [technique] has been...imaging or visualization."[9]

Film

Remember Yoda from the Star Wars films? In *The Empire Strikes*

Back, he instructed young Luke Skywalker, "You must feel the Force around you. Here, between you and me. Between the rock...everywhere. Yes, even the land." This language matches the teachings found in popular New Age writings. A study of today's popular films reveals many references that have their origin in New Age beliefs.

Psychology

The human potential movement is a natural outgrowth of the New Age worldview. We are taught that we are our own god, and we can create our own reality. Empowerment is the key to success, through affirmations (positive self-talk) and visualization (mental pictures of what we want to create). This is in clear contrast with the Bible's teaching that there is one true God who controls everything that happens in the universe.

Ethics

Because everything is one, there are no moral wrongs and rights. Everything is relative. We all create our own destiny—even victims of crime. When the acting teacher of Shirley MacLaine's daughter was burned beyond recognition in a head-on collision, MacLaine wondered, "Why did she choose to die that way?" Reincarnation and karma will bring about justice in the end. The Bible, however, is clear that certain actions are either right or wrong. It provides a clear standard for human morals.

Politics

Many New Age adherents believe a one-world government is necessary to recognize the oneness of humanity. Political agenda items often include ecological conservation, nuclear disarmament, relieving overpopulation and starvation, transcending the masculine and feminine distinctions in society, and redistributing wealth on a global level.

Education

Many textbooks that have removed references to Christianity now include New Age ideas and practices—among them being Eastern meditation, Indian spirituality, yoga, chanting, and visualization.

Business

The business world has embraced the human potential movement in the hopes of increasing productivity, fostering better employee relations, and bringing greater sales. Seminars help participants create their own reality and realize their unlimited potential.[10]

Common New Age Practices

Below are listed some of the common practices in the New Age movement with a brief description about each. For additional information about the Bible's teachings on these teachings and practices, go to www.johnankerberg.org and see the section on New Age.

Channeling

A method by which the spirit of a dead individual is summoned. Channelers usually try to make contact with a single spiritually evolved being. That being's consciousness is channeled through the medium and relays guidance and information to the group through the use of the medium's voice. Perhaps the most famous result of channeling is the popular book *A Course in Miracles*. It was channeled through a Columbia University psychologist, Dr. Helen Schucman (1909–1981), over an eight-year period. She was an atheist, and in no way regarded herself as a New Age believer. However, she took great care in recording accurately the words that she said she received from another source.

According to the Bible, channeling is specifically forbidden (Deuteronomy 18:9-12). The hidden purpose of the spirits is to gain the confidence of people so they can influence and control them to bring their eventual spiritual ruin (see 2 Corinthians 4:4).[11]

Crystals

Crystals are minerals that have their molecules arranged in a specific, highly ordered internal pattern. This pattern is reflected in the crystal's external structure, which typically has symmetrical planar surfaces. Many common substances, from salt to sugar, form crystals, as well as quartz and diamonds. They can be shaped so that they will vibrate at a specific frequency and are widely used in radio communications and computing devices. New Age practitioners say that crystals possess healing energy or powers. However, the Bible prohibits the usage of crystals to receive spiritual energy, as this is a common practice of pagan religions.[12]

Meditation

From a New Age perspective, meditation involves blanking out the mind and releasing oneself from conscious thinking. This process is often aided by repetitive chanting of a mantra, or by focusing on an object in order to enter a mystical state, or by a feeling of peace and oneness with the universe. This is quite different from biblical prayer and meditation, in which a person's thoughts focus upon God and seek his will. In Christian meditation, a person prays to ask for God's help, then listens for him to respond through God's Word, the Bible.

New Age Music

New age music is usually gentle, melodic, and inspirational, and typically involves the human voice, a harp, a lute, a flute, and other similar instruments. This music is used as an aid in healing, massage therapy, and general relaxation. Many music retailers have a New Age section in their stores.

Divination

Divination involves the use of various objects or techniques to supposedly foretell the future, including the *I Ching,* pendulum movements, runes, and tarot cards. In the Bible, divination is rejected by name (Deuteronomy 18:9-12) as an involvement with spiritistic powers (Hosea 4:12; Acts 16:16-19). In certain ways, New Age or pagan divination is the occult counterpart to biblical prophecy.[13]

Astrology

Astrology has to do with the belief that the orientation of the planets at the time of one's birth and the location of one's birth predicts that individual's future and personality. Belief in astrology is common amongst New Age adherents, yet is not limited to them.[14]

Holistic Health

Among other things, holistic health teaches healing techniques that diverge from the traditional, scientific medical models for health care and improvement. These techniques are said to help cure disorders of the mind, body, and spirit and to promote wholeness and balance in the individual. Holistic health practices include acupuncture, crystal healing, homeopathy, iridology, massage, various meditation methods, polarity therapy, psychic healing, therapeutic touch, and reflexology.[15]

New Age Beliefs

Because the New Age movement does not have a creed or set system of religious beliefs, only the more basic and popular beliefs can be contrasted with the beliefs in Christianity. We've provided a short list here using our foundations of biblical Christianity.

A more comprehensive list on New Age and Spiritistic beliefs can be found in the Appendix.

Belief	New Age Perspective	Biblical Perspective
God	God is all and all is God. All is one. God is an impersonal force, or consciousness, or energy.	One God in three persons—Father, Son, and Holy Spirit.
Holy Book	The Bible contains hidden or secret meanings—especially the sayings of Jesus. Only some see these secret meanings. The Bible supports New Age.	Only the 66 books of the Holy Bible are the authoritative works of Christianity.

	Revelation has also come through other religious leaders (Buddha, Krishna, etc.). Revelations continue to be received from disembodied humans, UFOs, and spirit guides such as astrologers.	
Sin	People are basically good.	All people have sinned (except Jesus).
Jesus Christ	Jesus was a mere human, but he became the Christ. Some believe he went as a child to the East to learn from Hindu gurus and holy men. Jesus is an enlightened "way-shower," on par with Buddha, Krishna, and Zoroaster.	God's perfect son, holy, resurrected, divine (second person of the Trinity), yet also fully human.
Salvation	People don't have a sin problem; they are simply ignorant of their divinity. They don't need salvation from sin. Therefore, Jesus did not die to provide salvation from sin.	Obtained only by God's grace through faith in Jesus Christ, not by human effort.
Afterlife	Through reincarnation, a person is eventually "reunited" with God. Hell does not exist.	At death, all people will enter heaven or hell based on whether they have salvation in Jesus Christ. The Bible does not support reincarnation, annihilation (ending of the soul), or the existence of purgatory.

The New Age movement ultimately promotes a "whatever works" attitude that combines elements of spiritistic practices both ancient and modern for its own purposes. Many of its ideas have existed in other religions and at other times, so it is not truly new, but its ideas have attracted many followers.

The Bible says there is another explanation for the mystical experiences, out-of-body trips, and "healings" that occur in the New Age movement. It clearly teaches that Satan can come to humans disguised as an angel of light to deceive them (2 Corinthians 11:14). Evil spirits or demons are often called "deceiving spirits"—the apostle Paul wrote, "The Spirit clearly says that in later times some will abandon the faith and follow deceiving spirits and things taught by demons" (1 Timothy 4:1).

So according to the Bible, there are people who follow teachings given by demons. We believe some of these are found in New Age teachings about God, Jesus, sin, hell, and moral absolutes. Christians are told:

> Dear friends, do not believe every spirit, but test the spirits to see whether they are from God, because many false prophets have gone out into the world. This is how you can recognize the Spirit of God: Every spirit that acknowledges that Jesus Christ has come in the flesh is from God, but every spirit that does not acknowledge Jesus is not from God (1 John 4:1-3).

During the same television interview mentioned at the beginning of this chapter, I (John) asked Dr. Kubler-Ross if she believed there was an evil power in the world called Satan. She said yes. I then asked her if she thought Satan was so bad that he would give her a complete physical healing (which she had received through a spirit guide) to ultimately deceive her and separate her from God forever. She said she didn't think Satan was that bad! I explained to her that the Bible teaches that Satan and his demonic angels are just such beings.

Later in that same program I also interviewed Dr. Maurice Rawlings, a cardiologist. Dr. Rawlings was once an atheist who thought all religion was false. That all changed one day when he was examining a man who was having chest pains. According to our interview, he shared, "He was getting the pain while he was hooked to an EKG and if the EKG goes haywire, it's his heart. If it doesn't, it's not. But while we were examining him, he dropped dead instead.

"So I started to resuscitate him. Half the people that die unexpectedly will come back, if you know how to do it, with bare hands.

So I was working on this fellow, doing external heart massage, and mouth-to-mouth breathing, but he had a heart block. Sixty percent of our patients won't live till they get to the hospital because they get a rhythm disturbance and they die with heart stoppage before they get the heart attack. That's what happened to him.

"So I had to pass a pacemaker wire down the collarbone vein into his heart while he was on the floor, so he could overcome the heart block and respond to the resuscitation. Here I was, trying to do two things at once. When I would reach for something, he would die once more. He would roll his eyes up, sputter, turn blue, stop breathing, his heart would stop beating, and he would die clinically once more. I'd reach over and start him up again.

"It's a clinical death. We are talking about something you can resuscitate. We're not talking about biologic death, which will occur four minutes after the heartbeat ceases. The brain will die. Rigor mortis sets in. That is biologic death. It requires a resurrection. We don't resurrect anybody. We resuscitate them.

"But this fellow kept saying something that I didn't expect. He said, 'Doctor, I'm in hell! I'm in hell!' What do you do if you're the doctor? I told him to keep his hell to himself. I was busy saving his life. I didn't want to be contaminated with spiritual things.

"Then the nurses wanted me to do something. What would you do? I'm a heart specialist, not a minister. But finally I did something. It was a stupid thing. I said a prayer for him because he wanted me to help keep him out of hell. He said, 'Every time you let go of me, I go back to hell.'

"So I said, 'Say this prayer after me.' Here I am resuscitating this guy, blood spurting. He repeated after me, 'I believe Jesus Christ is the son of God. If I die, please take me to heaven. If I live, I'm yours. I'm on the hook forever.' I remember that part because I don't say prayers well. And he's been a strong Christian ever since. This little prayer, this amusing little prayer, was a religious conversion experience for this man. After he said that prayer, he had subsequent clinical deaths and he wasn't frightened anymore. He was quiet, peaceful. He was not afraid of dying anymore. This fellow had a religious conversion experience right there in my office. But the thing that I didn't count on was this amusing little prayer backfired and got me, too. I became a Christian."

Dr. Rawlings went on to tell me that he started cataloging his patients' good and bad "at death" experiences. Some 300 of his patients had hell experiences, and about 150 had heaven experiences. What made the difference? Those who had entrusted themselves to Jesus and asked him to forgive their sins had heaven experiences. Those who hadn't—even those who attended church—found themselves in hell. That was a very interesting interview. I'll always remember one statement Dr. Rawlings made. He said, "As an atheistic cardiologist, I began to see that the evidence showed me it wasn't safe to die."

What about you? Do you know where you will go the moment you die? If you are uncertain, we would encourage you to turn to our final chapter to discover what God says about knowing for sure that he will take you to heaven.

The New Age movement promotes an alternative worldview that has attracted many people with an interest in spiritual matters. But what about those at the other extreme—those who believe there is no God at all? In the next chapter, we will look at what agnostics and atheists believe about God, and compare their views to the foundational beliefs of biblical Christianity.

How Can Someone Have a Religion Without God?

13

"The idea of a personal God is quite alien to me and seems even naive."

—RICHARD DAWKINS, IN *THE GOD DELUSION*[1]

"Imagine the consequences if any significant component of the U.S. government actually believed that the world was about to end and that its ending would be glorious. The fact that nearly half of the American population apparently believes this, purely on the basis of religious dogma, should be considered a moral and intellectual emergency."

—SAM HARRIS, IN *LETTER TO A CHRISTIAN NATION*[2]

n a day when over 90 percent of Americans believe in some sort of higher power, atheism (the belief that there is no God) has recently become alive again at the popular level. With new bestselling titles such as *god Is Not Great, The God Delusion, Letter to a Christian Nation, The End of Faith,* and *God: The Failed Hypothesis* getting a lot of media attention from National Public Radio, *Newsweek, The New York Times,* Fox News, MSNBC, and even the Comedy Channel, atheism has again become mainstream news.

For example, one *Wall Street Journal* article observed:

> Indeed, the atheists are now looking to turn the tables: They want to make belief itself not simply an object of intellectual derision but a cause for personal embarrassment. A new generation of publicists for atheism has emerged to tell Americans in particular that we should be ashamed to retain a majority of religious believers, that in this way we resemble the benighted, primitive peoples of the Middle East, Africa and South America instead of the enlightened citizens of Western Europe.[3]

On the other hand, as *Christianity Today* has noted, "atheism is in trouble."[4] Why? The very media organizations that Christians often dismiss as liberal are dosing out plenty of negative sound bites regarding atheism's new expression of intolerance toward religion. One *New York Times* review of Dawkins's *The God Delusion,* for instance, notes, "Shirking the intellectual hard work, Dawkins prefers to move on to parodic 'proofs' that he has found on the internet."[5]

Agnosticism (agnostics say they do not know if there is a God) has not attracted the same kind of attention in the media, yet there are many today who subscribe to it.

According to recent surveys, about seven percent of Americans call themselves either atheists or agnostics. This means America has more atheists and agnostics than Mormons (by a 3 to 1 margin), Jews (by a 4 to 1 margin), or Muslims (by a 14 to 1 margin).[6]

In our time together in this chapter, we'll take a look at each of these "no God" religions, discuss the varieties of atheistic and agnostic viewpoints, and consider their most common arguments.

All About Agnosticism

"My view is that if there is no evidence for it, then forget about it. An agnostic is somebody who doesn't believe in something until there is evidence for it, so I'm an agnostic."

—CARL SAGAN[7]

Agnosticism is simply a belief that we can neither prove nor disprove the existence of God. The term was invented by Thomas Henry Huxley in 1869 to explain the religious attitude of those who claim that God cannot be proven or disproved.[8] Literally, agnosticism is *a* (without) and *gnosis* (knowledge). In other words, to be agnostic is to believe there is a lack of knowledge regarding the existence of a God or gods.

How Many?

The 2001 Canadian census data showed that the number percentage of "Atheists, Agnostics, Humanists, adherents of no religion, etc." rose from 12.3 percent in 1991 to 16.2 percent in 2001.[9]

The Varieties of Agnosticism

While agnosticism is considered one distinct worldview, there are several varieties of agnosticism in existence today. Nearly ten different types have been identified:

1. *Strong agnosticism*—the view that the question of the existence or nonexistence of God(s) is unknowable by nature or that human beings are ill-equipped to judge the evidence.

2. *Weak agnosticism*—the view that the existence or nonexistence of God(s) is currently unknown but is not necessarily unknowable; therefore, one will withhold judgment until more evidence is available.

3. *Apathetic agnosticism*—the view that there is no proof of either the existence or nonexistence of God(s), but since any God(s) that may exist appear unconcerned for the universe or the welfare of its inhabitants, the question is largely academic anyway.

4. *Non-practicing agnosticism*—the view that there is no

proof of either the existence or non-existence of God(s), and that it's meaningless to care.

5. *Ignosticism*—the view that the concept of God(s) is meaningless because it has no verifiable consequences.

6. *Agnostic theism*—the view of those who do not claim to personally know the existence of God(s), but still believe in such an existence.

7. *Agnostic spiritualism*—the view that there may or may not be a God or gods, while maintaining a general personal belief in a spiritual aspect of reality, particularly without a distinct religious basis or adherence to any established doctrine.

8. *Relative agnosticism*—this is similar to agnostic spiritualism, but adds the thought that if it were empirically proven that God or gods do or do not exist, it would not affect the beliefs of the relative agnostic.

9. *Agnostic atheism*—the view of those who do not know of the existence or nonexistence of God(s), and do not believe in God(s).[10]

Did you know there were so many ways to doubt God's existence? Most people don't. Let's look next at some famous agnostics.

Famous Agnostics

Agnostics have influenced the fields of science, literature, media, and philosophy. Perhaps the five most well-known agnostic thinkers are:[11]

- *Charles Darwin:* A nineteenth-century British geologist and founder of Darwinism and the theory of evolution. He wrote about his faith in two places in his book *Life and Letters:*

  The mystery of the beginning of all things is insoluble by us; and I for one must be content to remain an Agnostic.

I think an Agnostic would be the more correct description of my state of mind. The whole subject [of God] is beyond the scope of man's intellect.

- *Thomas H. Huxley:* A well-known English religious skeptic, he invented the term *agnostic* in the mid-nineteenth century. In 1899, he wrote:

  In matters of the intellect do not pretend that conclusions are certain which are not demonstrated or demonstrable. That I take to be the agnostic faith, which if a man keep whole and undefiled, he shall not be ashamed to look the universe in the face, whatever the future may have in store for him.

  When I reached intellectual maturity, and began to ask myself whether I was an atheist, a theist, or a pantheist; a materialist or an idealist; a Christian or a freethinker, I found that the more I learned and reflected, the less ready was the answer; until at last I came to the conclusion that I had neither art nor part with any of these denominations, except the last...So I took thought, and invented what I conceived to be the appropriate title of "agnostic."[12]

- *Robert G. Ingersoll:* Probably the most famous American agnostic of the nineteenth century. He commented on the problem of theodicy—why is evil present in a universe that was created and is run by God? In his opinion:

- The man who, without prejudice, reads and understands the Old and New Testaments will cease to be an orthodox Christian. The intelligent man who investigates the religion of any country without fear and without prejudice will not and cannot be a believer.[13]

- *Bertrand Russell:* Russell was a popular twentieth-century British philosopher who wrote the book *Why I Am Not a Christian.* He was arrested during World War I for antiwar activities. While filling out a form at the jail, he defined his religious affiliation as agnostic. An officer asked about this, and Russell said, "Ah yes; we all worship Him in our own way, don't we." This comment allegedly "kept him smiling through his first few days of incarceration."[14]

- *Voltaire:* This eighteenth-century French author and playwright is often considered the father of agnosticism. He once wrote that "Christianity is the most ridiculous, the most absurd and bloody religion that has ever infected the world."[15]

Christian philosopher and scholar Dr. Norman Geisler has this to say about agnosticism:

> Complete agnosticism is self-defeating; it reduces to the self-destructing assertion that "one knows enough about reality in order to affirm that nothing can be known about reality." This statement provides within itself all that is necessary to falsify itself. For if one knows something about reality, then he surely cannot affirm in the same breath that all of reality is unknowable. And of course if one knows nothing whatsoever about reality, then he has no basis whatsoever for making a statement about reality. It will not suffice to say that his knowledge about reality is purely and completely negative, that is, he is totally devoid of a knowledge of the "that." It follows that total agnosticism is self-defeating because it assumes some knowledge about reality in order to deny any knowledge of reality.[16]

Can a person be both an agnostic *and* an atheist?

According to some, the answer is yes. For example:

> In the end, the fact of the matter is a person isn't faced with the necessity of only being either an atheist or an agnostic. Quite the contrary, not only can a person be both, but it is in fact common for people to be both agnostics and atheists. An agnostic atheist won't

claim to know for sure that nothing warranting the label "god" exists or that such cannot exist, but they also don't actively believe that such an entity does indeed exist.[17]

All About Atheism

"The greatest question of our time is not communism versus individualism; not Europe versus America; not even the East versus West. It is whether men can live without God."

—WILL DURANT[18]

Atheism may be a minority religious view, but it's a very vocal one. The new atheism of today's media can be found in today's news, television, popular books, and even eBay (see sidebar below). But what is atheism?

While definitions vary, a general definition can be found in the word itself. *A* (without) and *theos* (God), simply defines atheism as the belief that there is no God. Whereas agnosticism believes God may or may not exist, atheism claims to "know" that there is no God in this world or the next.

The eBay Atheist

Are you looking for new people to attend your church? Try eBay. In January 2006, DePaul University graduate student and committed atheist Hemant Mehta made himself available on the auction site. Mehta promised to attend one hour of church for every ten dollars of the final bid.

OfftheMap.org purchased Mehta's services for $504 and sent Mehta, on assignment, to churches throughout the Chicago area. With an open mind, an outsider's perspective, and a dose of humor, Hemant has been reporting his findings on Off the Map's "Atheist Blog."[19]

Varieties of Atheism

Dr. Norman Geisler defines five general types of atheism:

1. *Traditional (metaphysical) atheism:* Holds that there never was, is, or will be a God. Those who have held this view include Ludwig Feuerbach, Karl Marx, Jean-Paul Sartre, and Antony Flew (before his conversion to theism).

Not All Atheists Stay Atheists

World-renowned scholar Dr. Antony Flew, the world's foremost philosophical atheist, recently announced his belief in God. His new book, *There Is a God,* highlights how his friendship with C.S. Lewis and numerous debates with Christian scholars influenced his philosophical change.

In fact, I (John) invited Dr. Antony Flew and Christian theologian Dr. Gary Habermas to appear on *The John Ankerberg Show* to debate the evidence for the existence of God, and more specifically, the evidence for the resurrection of Jesus from the dead (the three-hour debate can be ordered at john ankerberg.org). After the debate, conversations continued between myself, Habermas, and Flew. Later, we also published a book together called *Did Jesus Rise from the Dead?*

Then, in April 2004, Flew informed Dr. Habermas that he simply "had to go where the evidence leads." As a result of the traditional philosophical and scientific arguments offered by theists, he felt compelled to change from atheism to theism.

2. *Mythological atheism:* Writers such as Friedrich Nietzsche believe the God-myth was never an actual being, but was once a live model by which people lived. This God-myth has been killed by the advancement of man's understanding and culture.

3. *Semantical atheism:* Claims that God-talk is dead. This view was held by Paul van Buren and others influenced by the logical positivists, who had seriously challenged the meaningfulness of language about God. Of course, those who hold this latter view need not be actual atheists at all. They can admit to the existence of God and yet believe that it is not possible to talk about him in

meaningful terms. This view has been called *acognosticism* because it denies that we can speak of God in cognitive or meaningful terms.

4. *Conceptual atheism:* Believes that there is a God, but he is hidden from view, obscured by our conceptual constructions.

5. *Practical atheism:* Confesses that God exists but believes that we should live as if he does not. The point is that we should not use God as a crutch for our failure to act in a spiritual and responsible way.[20]

The Arguments of Atheism

Identifying the Arguments

The arguments in favor of atheism are largely negative, although some can be cast in positive terms. The negative arguments fall into two categories: arguments against proofs for God's existence, and arguments against God's existence. For the first set of arguments most atheists draw heavily on the skepticism of Hume and the agnosticism of Kant. For the second set, atheists offer what they consider to be good and sufficient reasons for believing no God exists. Among them are these:

1. the fact of evil
2. the apparent purposelessness of life
3. random occurrence in the universe
4. the First Law of Thermodynamics—that "energy can neither be created nor destroyed"—is cited as evidence that the universe is eternal and needs no Creator

Responding to the Arguments

How can one respond to the atheists' reasons for believing no God exists?

The Existence of Evil: Concerning the presence of evil in the world, the atheist's reasoning is circular. Former atheist C.S. Lewis argued that in order to know there is injustice in the world, one has to have a standard of justice. So, to effectively eliminate God via evil, one has to posit an ultimate moral standard by which to pronounce God evil. Theists argue that God is the ultimate moral standard because there cannot be an ultimate moral law without an Ultimate Moral Lawgiver.

Atheists respond that an absolutely good God must have a good purpose for everything, but there is no good purpose for much of the evil in the world. Hence, there cannot be an absolutely perfect God.

Theists point out that just because we do not know the purpose of evil occurrences does not mean that there is no good purpose. This argument does not necessarily disprove God; it only proves our ignorance of God's plan. Just because we do not see a purpose for all evil now does not mean we never will. The atheist is premature in his judgment. According to theism, a day of justice is coming. If there is a God, he must have a good purpose for evil, even if we do not know it yet. For a theist, God is omniscient and knows everything. He is omnibenevolent and has a good reason for everything. So, by his very nature he must have a good reason for evil.

The Assumption of Purposelessness: In assuming that life is without purpose, the atheist is again both a presumptuous and premature judge. How does one know there is no ultimate purpose in the universe? Just because an atheist cannot discern real purpose for life personally does not mean that God lacks any such purpose. Most people have experienced things in their lives that made no sense at the time they occurred, but eventually, in hindsight, seemed to have great purpose.

The Seemingly Random Universe: Seeming randomness in the universe does not disprove God. Further, some randomness is only apparent, not real. When DNA was first discovered it was believed that it split randomly. Now the entire scientific world knows the incredible design involved in the splitting of the double helix molecule known as DNA. Even seeming randomness has an intelligent purpose. Molecules of carbon dioxide are exhaled randomly with molecules of oxygen, but for a good purpose. If they did not, we would inhale the same poisonous gases we have exhaled. And some of what seems to be waste may be the product of a purposeful process. For example, horse manure makes good fertilizer. According to the atheist's time scale, the universe has been absorbing and neutralizing very well all its "waste." So far as we know, little so-called waste is really wasted. Even if there is some waste, it may be a necessary byproduct of a good process in a finite world like ours, just like sawdust results from logging. This is evidence *for* the existence of God, not evidence *against* his existence.

The Eternality of Matter: Astrophysicist Richard Dawkins and others now believe that all matter, energy, space, and time came into existence when the big bang occurred approximately 13.8 million years ago. They say all this was brought about by a transcendent causal agent, and that this indicates that matter is *not eternal.*

Atheists often misstate the scientific First Law of Thermodynamics. It should not be rendered, "Energy can neither be created nor destroyed." Science, as science, should not be engaged in *can* or *cannot* statements. Operation science deals with what is or is not, based on observation. And observation simply tells us, according to the first law, that "the amount of actual energy in the universe remains constant." That is, while the amount of usable energy in the universe is decreasing, the amount of energy available is remaining constant. The first law says absolutely nothing about the origin or destruction of energy. It is merely an observation about the continuing presence of energy in the cosmos. If allowed to continue long enough, the sun will stop burning, the stars will go dark, and the universe will run down because of entropy, or the loss of usable energy. This also indicates that the universe had an original cause or start.

Comparing Atheism and Agnosticism with Christianity

As we consider these varied belief systems, we see once again the key differences that make these movements a "big deal" in comparison with biblical Christianity:

Belief	Agnostic/Atheistic Perspective	Biblical Perspective
God	God either does not exist or we don't know if he exists.	One God in three persons—Father, Son, and Holy Spirit.
Holy Book	No holy writings.	The 66 books of the Holy Bible are the authoritative works of Christianity.
Sin	Views vary, though most would agree that people sin or do wrong acts.	All people have sinned (except Jesus).
Jesus Christ	No consistent view other than that he is not God nor God's Son. He is usually considered a legend or common man.	God's perfect son, holy, resurrected, divine (second person of the Trinity), yet also fully human.
Salvation	Salvation does not exist because God does not exist.	Obtained only by God's grace through faith in Jesus Christ, not by human effort.
Afterlife	Unknown, though many believe a person's soul or spirit ceases to exist upon physical death.	At death, all people will enter heaven or hell based on whether they have salvation in Jesus Christ.

One of the key distinctions we find in these belief systems is a lack of purpose in this life or hope regarding the future. The logical arguments for agnosticism or atheism fail to convince. As C.S. Lewis once noted when he was still an atheist, "The world is filled with dreadful traps." That is, God has provided evidence that points to his existence. This evidence ranges all the way from the smallest particle of DNA to the vast universe, which exhibits over 200 finely tuned physical laws—the absence of any one of which would mean life could not exist anywhere in the universe. Further, the end result of these beliefs fails to satisfy. Why? According to Dr. Norman Geisler:

> Most nontheists claim they do not need God, but their own writings and experiences betray their position. But

if there is a real need for God, it is far more reasonable to believe that there is a real God who can really fill this real need.[21]

Ultimately, the Christian approach to those who claim to be agnostics or atheists is to lovingly present the rational evidence that refutes their arguments, present the person and claims of Jesus Christ, and offer hope for those who seek truth and positive change for their future.

Where Do
We Grow
Conclusion | from Here?

I f you've remained with us this far through the journey together, you are likely someone passionately desiring to really understand the big deal about other religions. Possibly your knowledge has increased and your concern has intensified regarding the importance of what you believe (or don't believe). If the comparisons and other evidence have led you to consider Christianity's leader, Jesus, as God's son, then what are the next steps to take?

To begin, your choice must be focused on the evidence, along with the possibility of experiencing a relationship with God through his son, Jesus. This process of getting to know Jesus includes the following acknowledgments:

First, as the Jewish prophet Isaiah confessed generations ago, "All of us, like sheep, have strayed away. We have left God's paths to follow our own."[1] Ever lied? Ever had an impure thought? Ever shouted an unkind word? We all have. God calls these unkind and hurtful actions sin. Our first step toward following Jesus is to acknowledge there is a God, and it's not us. Second, we need the help of a higher power, not a power found within ourselves.

We need to realize that our wrongful thoughts and actions hold severe consequences, according to the Bible. Isaiah penned the words,

"It's your sins that have cut you off from God."[2] Another Bible writer explains, "The person who sins is the one who will die."[3] To be candid about it, Jesus said our sins, no matter how great or small, separate us from experiencing and knowing God while we are alive here on Earth. If we continue, our sins will separate us eternally from God, and we will go to hell.[4] Though many don't like to talk about hell, it's a reality we cannot afford to ignore.

The good news is that the price to restore our broken relationship with God has already been arranged and paid for. The cost? Jesus' death on the cross. According to the prophets and apostles:

- "The LORD laid on him the sins of us all."[5]

- "He was pierced for our rebellion, crushed for our sins. He was beaten so we could be whole. He was whipped so we could be healed."[6]

- "He bore the sins of many and interceded for rebels."[7]

- "Christ suffered for our sins once for all time. He never sinned, but he died for sinners to bring you safely home to God."[8]

Jesus said the primary reason he came into our world was to rescue us from divine judgment. Because all of us sin and stand before a holy God as sinners, we are therefore condemned. It does not matter whether you are a big sinner or small sinner. Just one sin, committed against an infinitely holy God, is enough to require infinite punishment.

Someone once asked Jesus, "Which is the greatest commandment in the Law?" Jesus answered that it is to love the Lord your God with all your heart and with all your soul and with all your mind (Matthew 22:36-37). Have you always loved God with all your heart, soul, and mind in every moment of your life? If not, then Jesus is explaining that you are guilty of breaking the greatest commandment of them all. And we've all done that.

What's the answer to our dilemma? Jesus promised we could have our wrongs fully and freely forgiven. We can have our guilt removed, our joy restored, and experience a daily relationship with God. To enjoy these benefits, we are called to accept the challenge to turn away from our wrongs, to ask for forgiveness (an act of humility), and to trust in Jesus as our Lord and Savior (an act of faith). How can we know this? From the most primitive times, the writers of God's Word have communicated:

> Seek the LORD while you can find him. Call on him now while he is near. Let the wicked change their ways and banish the very thought of doing wrong. Let them turn to the LORD that he may have mercy on them. Yes, turn to our God, for he will forgive generously.[9]

Jesus promised, "I tell you the truth, those who listen to my message and believe in God who sent me have eternal life. They will never be condemned for their sins, but they have already passed [at that moment] from death into life..."[10] In a prayer to his father the night before his crucifixion, Jesus shared, "This is the way to have eternal life—to know you, the only true God, and Jesus Christ, the one you sent to earth."[11]

The best part about what Jesus offers is that it's not based on the quality of our performance—in fact, it's not based on our performance at all. Jesus certainly wants us to do what is right, but following him is based on his gift of grace, not upon our good works. Our part is to take the step of faith and receive this life-changing gift.

Paul, the great missionary and apostle, described this mystery, writing to early Christ-followers that "God saved you by his grace when you believed. And you can't take credit for this; it is a gift from God. Salvation is not a reward for the good things we have done, so none of us can boast about it."[12]

You will learn that the big deal about Jesus that separates him from other gods is his great love for us. He has done all of the work already and invites us to embrace him in an intimate relationship for all eternity. Are you ready to enter this relationship with Jesus? Will you choose the way of Jesus?

There is no set prayer for starting the journey, but we'd like to offer a model to help guide you. If you don't know where to begin, start with this:

> God, I ask your son Jesus to enter my life as my leader and rescuer. I know I've messed up and can never save myself. Please forgive me. I believe Jesus died for all my sins and came back to life from the dead and is living now. I now place my total faith in him for eternal life. I choose to follow Jesus from this moment forward. Please strengthen me and show me how to live for you.

If you have just made this commitment, congratulations! We can remember the day when we each believed and opened ourselves to Jesus. Your life will never be the same. You will experience forgiveness, love, joy, and a peace through life's ups and downs. If you're coming back to begin afresh with Jesus, you can rest assured there is no one he will turn away. We want to encourage you to take that step and renew your spiritual journey as well. No matter where you've been, Jesus wants to help you move forward on an adventure of faith.

We also invite you to let us know about any decision you have made or new growth you have experienced. Please email us at big dealaboutotherreligions@johnankerberg.org with your story. We'll be thrilled to share with you about additional resources for spiritual growth. Allow us the privilege of enjoying together your decision to make the newfound relationship with Jesus the relationship that supersedes all others in your life.

Biblical Warnings Against Occult Involvement

By Dr. John Ankerberg
and Dr. John Weldon[1]

hether or not practitioners accept the categories, the data point unmistakably to the conclusion that the essence of occult practice constitutes a trafficking with demons. From this reality flows a number of other concerns: idolatry, spiritual deception, the likelihood of possession, psychological and physical harm, and the immoral, ethically consequential teachings that inevitably accompany demonic involvement or revelations. Our purpose is to simply document that God does indeed warn against the occult.

God teaches that spiritual warfare is a reality (Ephesians 6:10-18; 2 Corinthians 2:11; 1 Peter 5:8) and that supernatural manifestations are not to be accepted uncritically but to be tested by the Word of God (1 John 4:1; Revelation 2:2; Acts 17:10-12; Deuteronomy 18:20-22; Matthew 24:24, etc.). Scripture also speaks of the reality of a personal devil and myriads of demons who should be regarded as cunning enemies of both the believer in Christ and the nonbeliever (John 8:44; 13:27; Matthew 6:13; 9:34; 12:24; Luke 8:12; 13:16; 2 Corinthians 4:4; Colossians 1:13; 2 Thessalonians 2:9; Acts 16:16-18; 2 Corinthians 2:11; 11:3; 2 Timothy 2:26). Indeed, one of the devil's tactics is to masquerade as an "angel of light" and a servant of righteousness (2 Corinthians 11:13-15).

The Scripture also warns that false prophets are linked to evil spirits and that there are "doctrines of demons" (1 John 4:1; 1 Timothy 4:1); that there is great power in the occult (Isaiah 47:9); that Satan is the god of this world (2 Corinthians 4:4); that the whole world lies in the power of this evil one (1 John 5:19); that demons work through people by giving them psychic abilities (Acts 16:16-19; Exodus 7:11,22; 8:7); and that Satan and his hordes are active in the affairs of the planet (Ephesians 2:2; Daniel 10:12-13,20).

In many instances, Scripture explicitly cites Satan or his demons as the reality behind occult involvement, idolatry, and false religion (Deuteronomy 32:16-17; 1 Corinthians 10:19-21; Psalm 106:35-40; 1 Timothy 4:1; 2 Thessalonians 2:9-10; Acts 16:16-19). This is one reason God considers occult activity, in virtually all its forms, as an abomination (Deuteronomy 18:9-12)—because it links those for whom Christ died to evil spirits, who are his enemies. Thus, occult involvement will eventually lead to judgment for those who refuse to forsake it (Revelation 22:15; 2 Chronicles 33:6).

Scripture condemns by name spiritism, mediumism, and necromancy (Deuteronomy 18:9-12; 2 Chronicles 33:2-3,6); various forms of sorcery and divination (Deuteronomy 18:9-12; Hosea 4:12; Exodus 22:18; Isaiah 44:25; 29:8-9; Ezekiel 21:21; e.g., astrology, Deuteronomy 17:2-5; 2 Kings 17:15-17; Isaiah 47:9-14); and magic (Acts 13:8; 19:16-19; Isaiah 47:9,12).

In their numerous forms, these basic categories (magic, spiritism, divination, and sorcery) cover almost the entire gamut of occult activity. But the irreducible reality of all occultism is spiritism. Thus:

> [Spiritism]...is one of the oldest known forms of religious expression. It is also one of the deadliest where the certainty of divine judgment is concerned...It is terminal error, since it demonstrates not only an active rejection of God, but an active embrace of his replacement. It is, as

the prophets put it, "spiritual adultery," carried to completion. It is faithlessness fulfilled.

The extent to which a society endorses or indulges in widespread spiritism, therefore, is something of a spiritual thermometer. It can give us a rough estimate of our collective state of spiritual health...The Bible levies its judgment against spiritism at two levels. It treats spiritism as a symptom of social decline as well as an act of personal culpability.

All sin provokes God's judgment. Advanced or developed sin provokes it more directly and immediately. As a social symptom, spiritism represents the final stage of a long process of spiritual decay. It is the terminal phase of our flight from God. It is terminal because God's judgment on spiritism is not meant to admonish or correct, but to cleanse and extirpate.

On an individual scale, the practice of spiritism is terminal because it represents an ultimate confusion of values. It trades humanity's privilege of intimacy with God for sheer fascination with a liar who secretly hates all that is human and all that humans hold dear.[2]

In over 20 years of studying spiritistic contacts and literature and the effects of these on the lives of spiritists, we can confirm this view wholeheartedly.

Clearly, Scripture warns against the occult. And just as clearly, those who practice it disobey what God's Word commands. In essence, occult activity courts deception and betrayal from the demonic realm as well as judgment from God for engaging in it, and thereby promotes spiritual evil under the guise of legitimate religious practice.

Discussion Guide

These discussion questions are intended to facilitate further conversation between friends, within small groups, and among book club members, and church classmates. Please feel free to use them in whatever way helps you best grapple with the issues shared in this book. Greater understanding often results from the conversation itself rather than simply the bottom-line answer. For additional perspectives or other helpful resources, please see the "Additional Resources" section on page 235, or check out any of the numerous study tools available at www.johnankerberg.org.

Part One: Christianity and Roman Catholicism

1. Christianity: What's the Big Deal About Jesus?
   - Why do you think people say there is more than one way to God?
   - In your opinion, how strong is the evidence for the truthfulness of Christianity?
   - In what ways does Christianity stand or fall based on the resurrection of Jesus?

2. Roman Catholicism: The One True Church?
   - What do you consider the biggest difference between biblical Christianity and Roman Catholicism?

- Do you think Roman Catholicism differs from biblical Christianity? Why or why not?

- In what ways is biblical salvation good news to a person from a Roman Catholic background?

Part Two: Other One-God Religions

3. Judaism: Why Do Jews Get to Be God's Chosen People?
   - What are some of the different ways people define Judaism today (in terms of culture, beliefs, etc.)?

   - What foundational beliefs do Jews and Christians share? In what ways could these be helpful when talking about Jesus with a person of Jewish background?

   - Why do you think more Jews have not converted to Christianity? How could Christians better communicate their beliefs with those who hold to Jewish beliefs?

4. Islam: Is Allah Really the Only God?
   - Why do you think Islam is so popular around the world today?

   - How does investigating the history of Islam influence your thoughts regarding this religion?

   - What are some of the key differences of belief between Islam and biblical Christianity? What evidence about Jesus should be persuasive to Muslims?

Part Three: Popular Alternative Religions

5. Mormonism: Aren't Mormons Christians?
   - Do you think Mormons are Christians? Why or why not?

   - What attracts people to Mormonism? Why is this important to recognize?

   - How would a Christian talk to a Mormon about how to have a relationship with God?

6. Jehovah's Witnesses: What's with the Watchtower?

- What is the significance of Jehovah's Witnesses including, in their translation of the Bible, several changes that do not exist in the original languages?

- Why are Jehovah's Witnesses often highly motivated to practice their faith via involvement in door-to-door outreach and attendance at many Bible studies and meetings?

- What are some of the biggest differences between the beliefs of Jehovah's Witnesses and the teachings of the Bible? Why is the biblical gospel good news to Jehovah's Witnesses?

7. Wicca: Is Witchcraft for Real?

- What does the Bible teach regarding involvement in witchcraft that can apply toward Wicca? (Hint: See the appendix for verses relevant to this question.)

- Why is Wicca incompatible with Christian beliefs?

- How do people become involved in Wicca and other forms of witchcraft so easily today? What could you do to help avoid Wicca's negative influence?

8. Kabbalah: A Mystical Judaism?

- Why has Kabbalah grown in popularity?

- How does the involvement of celebrities help Kabbalah?

- What would you say to a Christian friend who felt Kabbalah practices were helpful to his or her spiritual growth?

Part Four: Eastern Religions

9. Hinduism: Everything Is One?

- Why is it significant that Hinduism has no known founder or universally accepted set of beliefs or holy writings? What do you think critics would say if the same were true of Christianity?

- In what ways do you find Hinduism difficult to relate to? Why do you think this is the case?

- Where do you see Hindu practices used in our culture today, such as in films or exercise? How do you think Christians should respond to these practices?

10. Buddhism: What's with the Enlightenment Thing?
- What is the appeal of reincarnation in Buddhist belief? How does this compare with what the Bible teaches regarding the afterlife?

- How is the Buddhist focus on personal enlightenment different from the pursuit of Christian spiritual growth?

- Where would you begin when discussing Jesus with someone from a Buddhist background?

11. Confucianism, Taoism, and Shintoism: What's with All the -isms?
- In what ways are these three -isms religions? In what ways do they seem only philosophies?

- Why do you think many people who practice Confucianism, Taoism, and Shinto practice more than one form of religion?

- How is biblical Christianity more relational than these -isms? In what ways could this relational aspect appeal to people who follow these philosophies?

Part Five: Multigod and Anti-God Religions

12. The New Age Movement: What's So New About New Age?
- In what ways does New Age religion resemble ancient pagan religions?

- What are some examples of New Age practices that are common in today's culture?

- How could you share your concerns with a New Age friend or family member, using Scripture from the Bible?

13. Agnosticism and Atheism: How Can Someone Have a Religion Without God?
   - How can agnosticism and atheism be considered religions when they do not believe God exists?

   - Why do you think many of today's writings on atheism have taken on a more spiteful, emotional tone?

   - What could you do to help a person who does not believe in God to sincerely investigate the evidence for God's existence?

Additional Resources

nterested in learning more? If you want more useful material, we've listed several excellent tools you can refer to. Below are some resources available from the Ankerberg Theological Research Institute, and a list of helpful Web sites. Please note that our mention of a resource does not necessarily mean we agree with that resource's contents. Those books and Web sites are listed because they are of a generally helpful nature.

Ankerberg Theological Research Institute Resources

All the following Ankerberg resources can be ordered online at www.johnankerberg.org or by calling (423) 892-7722.

Books

The following related books are coauthored by Dr. John Ankerberg and Dillon Burroughs:

> *Middle East Meltdown*
>
> *What's the Big Deal About Jesus?*
>
> *What Can Be Found in Lost?*

The following related books are coauthored by Dr. John Ankerberg and Dr. John Weldon:

> *Encyclopedia of New Age Religions*
>
> *The Facts on Halloween*
>
> *The Facts on Islam*

The Facts on Jehovah's Witnesses

The Facts on the Mormon Church

The Facts on Roman Catholicism

The Facts on World Religions

Fast Facts on Defending Your Faith

Fast Facts on Islam

Fast Facts on Jehovah's Witnesses

Fast Facts on Mormonism

Fast Facts on Roman Catholicism

The following related books are authored or coauthored by Dillon Burroughs:

Comparing Christianity with the Cults (Moody)

Comparing Christianity with World Religions (Moody)

Video Programs and Transcripts

The following resources are available in VHS and DVD formats. Most programs offer downloadable transcripts as well.

Agnosticism and Atheism

Christianity Under Attack: Debate on Christianity and Secular Humanism

Did Jesus Really Rise from the Dead?

The Search for Jesus

Why Do Bad Things Happen to Good People?

Christianity (comparative perspective):

From Skepticism to Belief—The Facts and Evidence that Can Lead You Step by Step to Belief in Christ

Islam:

Former Muslims Testify about Islam

How to Lead a Muslim to Christ

Islam and Christianity

What Do Muslims Believe?

Where Is Islam Taking the World?

Jehovah's Witnesses:

Ex-Jehovah's Witnesses Convention

Former Jehovah's Witnesses Testify

Has the Watchtower Ever Lied, Covered Up, or Changed
Important Doctrines, Dates, and Biblical Interpretations?

How to Witness to a Jehovah's Witness

Jesus, Salvation, and the Bible: What Do Mormons and
Jehovah's Witnesses Believe?

What You Need to Know When Jehovah's Witnesses Come
Knocking at the Door

Mormonism:

Former Mormons Testify

Jesus, Salvation, and the Bible: What Do Mormons and Jehovah's
Witnesses Believe?

Mormon Officials and Christian Scholars Compare Doctrine

Mormonism Revisited

The Truth about Mormonism

New Age:

America Looks Inward

Apostasy, Spiritism, and the Occult

Astrology: Do the Heavens Determine Your Destiny?

Modern Channeling and Spirit Guides

New Age Occultism and the Christian

The New Age Movement and the Church

Roman Catholicism:

> Do Roman Catholics and Evangelical Protestants Now Agree?
>
> Do Roman Catholics and Protestants Agree on Justification and Papal Infallibility?
>
> Do Roman Catholics and Protestants Agree on Maryology and Purgatory?
>
> Roman Catholicism and the Gospel

Online Articles

Over 2500 online articles on Christianity and comparative religions are hosted on the Ankerberg Theological Research Institute Web site. You can find more information about the religious groups discussed in this book at www.johnankerberg.org.

Helpful Websites

Some helpful Web sites about world religions from a Christian perspective include:

> www.adherents.com: Ever wondered how many people belong to a particular religious group? Adherents.com is your one-stop source for statistics on world religions.
>
> www.bible.org: Home of the NET Bible, this site offers thousands of articles on nearly every aspect of Bible study.
>
> www.biblegateway.com: Search the major English translations of the Bible by passage, key word, or topic.
>
> www.carm.org: Christian Apologetics and Resource Ministries provide a tremendous wealth of free resources on comparative religions, all written from a Christian perspective.
>
> www.leaderu.com: A ministry of Campus Crusade for Christ, LeaderU offers several links and articles on Christianity, ranging from entry level to academic.
>
> www.probe.org: This Christian media ministry offers numerous online articles and audio resources on Christianity and other religions.

www.ronrhodes.org: Reasoning from the Scriptures offers several online articles related to Christian evaluations of other religions.

www.trueu.org: The college-aged outreach of Focus on the Family, which provides several young-adult targeted articles on defending the faith.

Notes

Why Should I Care About Other Religions?

1. Larry King Live interview on February 16, 2006. Accessed at http://www.celebatheists.com/index.php?title=George_Clooney.
2. Cited at http://www.afajournal.org/2006/october/1006church.asp.
3. Cited at http://www.leaderu.com/wri/articles/paths.html.
4. John 18:38.
5. Gerald C. McDermott, *Can Evangelicals Learn from Other Religions?* (Downers Grove, IL: Intervarsity Press, 2000), p. 216.
6. Harold A. Netland, *Dissonant Voices* (Grand Rapids, MI: Eerdmans, 1991), p. 37.
7. Adapted from Steve Russo, "Don't All Spiritual Paths Lead to God?" *Breakaway* magazine, 2005. Accessed at http://www.breakawaymag.com/GodFaith/A000000013.cfm.
8. Netland, *Dissonant Voices*, p. 160.

Chapter 1—Christianity: What's the Big Deal About Jesus?

1. "A Biblical Worldview Has a Radical Effect on a Person's Life," December 1, 2003. Accessed at http://www.barna.org/FlexPage.aspx?Page=BarnaUpdate&BarnaUpdateID=154. Also, "Only Half of Protestant Clergy Have Biblical Worldview," January 12, 2004, accessed at http://www.barna.org/FlexPage.aspx?Page=BarnaUpdate&BarnaUpdateID=156.
2. Alister E. McGrath, *Intellectuals Don't Need God & Other Modern Myths* (Grand Rapids: Zondervan, 1993), p. 119.
3. John Ankerberg and John Weldon, *The Facts on World Religions* (Eugene, OR: Harvest House, 2004), p. 10.
4. For more on this see *What's the Big Deal About Jesus?* (Eugene, OR: Harvest House, 2007).

5. Norman Geisler, *Baker Encyclopedia of Christian Apologetics* (Grand Rapids, MI: Zondervan, 1999), p. 732.

6. Meaning "traditional" Protestant Christianity that continues to follow the Reformation principle of *sola scriptura*, or "only Scripture."

7. C. Stephen Evans, *Why Believe? Reason and Mystery as Pointers to God* (Grand Rapids: Eerdmans, 1996), p. 141.

8. John 8:46.

9. Matthew 20:28.

10. While some Christians today do not accept this teaching, it is the standard, traditional view. For a full statement about this, see the Chicago Statement on Biblical Inerrancy (which can be accessed at http://www.bible-researcher .com/chicago1.html), which also serves as the agreed-upon view for scholarly Christian societies such as the Evangelical Theological Society (www .etsjets.org).

11. Adapted from http://www.soon.org.uk/page19.htm.

12. Steve Russo, "Don't All Spiritual Paths Lead to God?" *Breakaway* magazine, 2005. Accessed at http://www.breakawaymag.com/GodFaith/A000000013 .cfm.

13. Ephesians 2:8-9 NLT.

Chapter 2—Roman Catholicism: The One True Church?

1. August Bernard Hasler, *How the Pope Became Infallible: Piux IX and the Politics of Persuasion* (Garden City, NY: Doubleday, 1981), p. 310.

2. *Catechism of the Catholic Church* (Liguori, MO: Liguori Publications, 1994), p. 315.

3. Ibid., p. 321.

4. Ibid., p. 312.

5. Ibid., p. 320.

6. Ibid.

7. Ibid., p. 324.

8. Ibid., p. 330.

9. Both citations, ibid., p. 351.

10. Ibid., p. 363.

11. Ibid., p. 381.

12. Ibid., p. 384.

13. Robert C. Broderick, ed., *The Catholic Encyclopedia*, rev. ed. (Nashville, TN: Thomas Nelson, 1987), p. 502.

14. From "Do Roman Catholics and Protestants Agree on Justification and Papal Infallibility?" on *The John Ankerberg Show*, 1985.

Part Two: Other One-God Religions

1. Accessed at http://www.adherents.com/Religions_By_Adherents.html.

Chapter 3—Judaism: Why Do Jews Get to Be God's Chosen People?

1. As cited in Bruce Bickel and Stan Jantz, *World Religions & Cults 101* (Eugene, OR: Harvest House Publishers, 2002), p. 39.

2. From http://www.adherents.com/Religions_By_Adherents.html. Some claim there are as many as 18 million Jews, though precise statistics are difficult to determine due to different ways of identification.

3. Bickel and Jantz, *World Religions & Cults 101*, p. 41.

4. *American Jewish Year Book 2005* (New York: American Jewish Committee, 2005), cited at the Jewish Virtual Library at http://www.jewishvirtuallibrary.org/jsource/Judaism/jewpop.html.

5. Adapted from the article "What Is Judaism?" accessed at http://www.jewfaq.org/judaism.htm.

6. Adin Steinsaltz, *We Jews: Who We Are and What Should We Do?* (New York: Jossey-Bass, 2005).

7. "Movements of Judaism" at http://www.jewfaq.org/movement.htm. Several smaller movements also exist, including Hasidism, Humanism, Reconstructionism, and Zionism.

8. "Messianic Judaism" at http://en.wikipedia.org/wiki/Messianic_Judaism#_note-0.

9. Cited in "What Do Jews Believe?" at http://www.jewfaq.org/beliefs.htm.

10. Adapted from material at http://www.religionfacts.com/islam/comparison_charts/islam_judaism_christianity.htm.

11. Pat Zukeran, "The Uniqueness of Jesus," Leadership University. Accessed at http://www.leaderu.com/orgs/probe/docs/unique.html.

12. Alfred Edersheim, *The Life and Times of Jesus the Messiah*, one-volume edition (Grand Rapids, MI: Eerdmans, 1972), p. 163. You can also view all 456 prophecies at http://www.levendwater.org/books/life_times_edersheim_appendix.pdf, pp. 59ff.

Chapter 4—Islam: Is Allah Really the Only God?

1. "Contemporary figures for Islam are usually between 1 billion and 1.8 billion, with 1 billion being a figure frequently given in comparative religion texts, probably because it's such a nice, round number." From http://www.adherents.com/Religions_By_Adherents.html#Islam.

2. Patrick Belton, "In the Way of the Prophet: Ideologies and Institutions in Dearborn, Michigan, America's Muslim Capitol," *The Next American City*, October 2003. Accessed at http://www.americancity.org/article.php?id_article=72.

3. Ergun Caner, "Where Is Islam Taking the World?" interview for *The John Ankerberg Show*, March 2006.

4. Cited in Josh McDowell, *A Ready Defense* (Nashville, TN: Thomas Nelson, 1992), p. 304.

5. See Josh McDowell, *A Ready Defense*, pp. 305-09.

6. "All About Islam." Accessed at http://www.simpletoremember.com/vitals/IslamJudaism.htm.

7. Adapted from Norman L. Geisler and Abdul Saleeb, *Answering Islam* (Grand Rapids, MI: Baker Books, 1993), pp. 293-94.

8. John Ankerberg and John Weldon, *The Facts on Islam* (Eugene, OR: Harvest House Publishers, 1998), p. 13.

9. Walid Pheres, *Future Jihad* (New York: Palgrave Macmillan, 2005) p. 45.

10. Ergun Caner, "Where Is Islam Taking the World?" interview for *The John Ankerberg Show,* March 2006 (emphasis added).

11. Adapted from Norm Geisler, "An Overview of Islamic Beliefs." Accessed at http://www.johnankerberg.org/Articles/islam/IS1200W2.htm.

12. Dr. Jamal Badawi, program one of the "Islam vs. Christianity" debate conducted by *The John Ankerberg Show.* Accessed at http://www.johnankerberg.org/Articles/islam/IS1299W2.htm.

13. A.J. Arberry, *The Koran Interpreted* (New York: MacMillan, 1976), p. 233.

14. Ibid., p. 315.

15. Ibid., p. 316.

16. Ibid., p. 317.

17. Ibid., p. 130.

18. Find the full article on this issue and supporting documentation in "How Do Muslims View Jesus Christ?" at http://www.johnankerberg.org/Articles/islam/IS1101W2.htm.

19. "Qur'an," accessed at http://en.wikipedia.org/wiki/Qur'an#The_Qur.27an_and_Islamic_culture.

20. Sura 23:104-05 in the George Sale translation (1734), as cited by Phillip H. Lochhaas, *How to Respond to Islam* (St. Louis: Concordia, 1981), p. 24.

21. N.J. Dawood, trans., *Koran* (New York: Penguin, 2000), p. 241.

22. Abdiyah Akbar Abdul-Haqq, *Sharing Your Faith with a Muslim* (Minneapolis: Bethany, 1980), p. 164.

23. John Ankerberg and John Weldon, "What Does Islam Teach About Salvation?" Accessed at http://www.johnankerberg.org/Articles/islam/IS1201W1.htm.

24. Several additional branches exist as well and can be found at "Divisions of Islam" at http://en.wikipedia.org/wiki/Divisions_of_Islam.

25. Emir Fethi Caner and Ergun Mehmet Caner, *More Than a Prophet: An Insider's Response to Muslim Beliefs About Jesus & Christianity* (Grand Rapids, MI: Kregel Publications, 2003), pp. 126-27.

Chapter 5—Mormonism: Aren't Mormons Christians?

1. From the LDS Newsroom at http://www.lds.org/newsroom/page/0,15606,4034-1---10-168,00.html. Based on 2005 statistics.

2. *Time,* August 4, 1997, p. 52.

3. *Times and Seasons* (Nauvoo, IL: 1839–46), 3: 728, 748.

4. *Times and Seasons* (Nauvoo, IL: 1839–46), 5: 613-14.

5. *Gospel Principles,* p. 52 (1992). Cited in "Authority of LDS Scriptures" at http://www.irr.org/MIT/WDIST/wdist-authority-of-lds-scriptures.html.

6. Helen Walters, "The Book of Mormon Today." Accessed at http://www.irr.org/mit/Book-of-Mormon-Today.html.

7. See "General Information FAQ" at http://www.utlm.org/faqs/faqgeneral.htm#6.

8. Full documentation of these prophecies is available in the article "Tips for Witnessing to Mormons." Accessed at http://www.contenderministries.org/mormonism/witnesstips.php.

9. "Joseph Smith Translation of the Bible," accessed at http://en.wikipedia.org/wiki/Joseph_Smith_Translation_of_the_Bible.

10. Adapted from an Ankerberg Theological Research Institute article written by James Bjornstad, "The Mormons—How Do Their Beliefs Regarding the Nature of God and Salvation Compare with Biblical Christianity?" Full documentation is provided for each topic. Accessed at http://www.johnankerberg.org/Articles/apologetics/AP0699W2.htm.

11. Ibid.

12. Kimberly Powell, "Why Do Mormons Research Their Ancestors?" Accessed at http://genealogy.about.com/od/church_records/f/mormons.htm.

Chapter 6—Jehovah's Witnesses: What's with the Watchtower?

1. Based on the most recent statistics from the "2005 Report of Jehovah's Witnesses." Accessed at http://www.watchtower.org/statistics/worldwide_report.htm.

2. See "Organizational Structure of Jehovah's Witnesses" at http://en.wikipedia.org/wiki/Organizational_structure_of_Jehovah%27s_Witnesses.

3. Edmond Gruss, *Apostles of Denial: An Examination and Expose of the History, Doctrines and Claims of the Jehovah's Witnesses* (Grand Rapids, MI: Baker, 1972), pp. 32-33, 219.

4. Bruce Metzger, "The Jehovah's Witnesses and Jesus Christ," rpt. of April 1953, *Theology Today* (Princeton, NJ: Theological Book Agency, 1953), p. 74.

5. *All Scripture Is Inspired By God and Beneficial* (WBTS, 1963), pp. 326, 327-30 (emphasis added).

6. *New World Translation of the Holy Scriptures* (WBTS, 1961), p. 5.

7. *The Kingdom Interlinear Translation of the Greek Scriptures* (WBTS, 1969), p. 5; *Reasoning From the Scriptures,* op. cit., p. 277, states, "We have not used any scholar's name for reference or recommendations because...the translation must be appraised on its own merits."

8. Julius Mantey, *Depth Exploration in the New Testament* (New York: Vantage Press, 1980), pp. 136-37.

9. "The Watchtower," at http://en.wikipedia.org/wiki/The_Watchtower.

10. "Awake!" at http://en.wikipedia.org/wiki/Awake!.

11. A complete listing of current Watchtower resources can be found at http://www.watchtower.org/e/publications/index.htm.

12. For a more detailed discussion of these differences, see the Ankerberg Theological Research Institute article "Jehovah's Witnesses" by James Bjornstad at http://www.johnankerberg.org/Articles/apologetics/AP0100W4.htm.

13. Genesis 40:20-22; Mark 6:21-27.

14. "Beliefs and Customs that Displease God." Accessed from the Watchtower website at http://www.watchtower.org/library/rq/article_11.htm.

15. Ibid.

16. "Blood—Vital for Life," from the Watchtower website at http://www.watchtower.org/library/hb/article_01.htm.

17. William and Joan Cetnar, *Questions for Jehovah's Witnesses* (William J. Cetnar: R.R. #3, Kunkletown, PA, 1983), p. 26; Duane Magnani, *Dialogue with a Jehovah's Witness*, vol. 2 (Clayton, CA: Witness, Inc.), pp. 368-374. For a refutation of this teaching, see Jerry Bergman, *Jehovah's Witnesses and Blood Transfusions* (St. Louis, MO: Personal Freedom Outreach, n.d.); Walter Martin, *Jehovah of the Watchtower* (Chicago: Moody Press, 1974), note 21, pp. 91-105.

Chapter 7—Wicca: Is Witchcraft for Real?

1. Denise Zimmermann and Katherine A. Gleason, revised with Miria Liguana, *The Complete Idiot's Guide to Wicca and Witchcraft*, 3rd ed. (New York: Alpha Books, 2006), p. 4.

2. American Religious Identification Survey 2001, City University of New York. Accessed at http://www.gc.cuny.edu/faculty/research_briefs/aris/key_findings.htm.

3. "Christians and Pagans Agree, Wicca Emerging as America's Third Religion," PRWeb, April 21, 2005. Accessed at http://www.emediawire.com/releases/2005/4/emw231351.htm.

4. Zimmermann and Gleason, *The Complete Idiot's Guide to Wicca and Witchcraft*, p. 3.

5. Ann-Marie Gallagher, *The Wicca Bible* (New York: Sterling Publishing Co., Inc., 2005), p. 16.

6. Zimmermann and Gleason, *The Complete Idiot's Guide to Wicca and Witchcraft*, p. 4.

7. Ibid., p. 24.

8. Zimmermann and Gleason, *The Complete Idiot's Guide to Wicca and Witchcraft*, p. 10.

9. A longer account of this history can be read in Hans Holzer's *The New Pagans* (New York: Doubleday, 1973).

10. The text of this case can be read at http://paganwiccan.about.com/gi/
dynamic/offsite.htm?zi=1/XJ/Ya&sdn=paganwiccan&cdn=religion&tm=3
0&gps=106_10_929_575&f=20&tt=14&bt=0&bts=0&zu=http%3A//www.
tangledmoon.org/dettmercase.htm.

11. See a list of these cases at http://www.totse.com/en/law/high_profile_legal_
cases/165203.html.

12. "A Nice Day for a Witch Wedding," *The Scotsman (Evening News)*, September 16, 2004.

13. Zimmermann and Gleason, *The Complete Idiot's Guide to Wicca and Witchcraft*, pp. 60-61.

14. Gary Cantrell, *Wiccan Beliefs and Practices* (Woodbury, MN: Llewellyn
Publications, 2006), p. 45.

15. Ibid., p. 48.

16. Gallagher, *The Wicca Bible*, p. 27.

17. From "Wicca" at http://en.wikipedia.org/wiki/Wicca.

18. Gallagher, *The Wicca Bible*, p. 27.

19. Direct quotes in this section, unless noted otherwise, are taken from the
website http://www.wicca.com.

20. Quotes from this section can be found in *Comparing Christianity with the
Cults* by Dillon Burroughs, Keith Brooks, and Irvine Robertson (Chicago,
IL: Moody Publishing, 2007).

21. Raven Grimassi, *The Wiccan Mysteries: Ancient Origins and Teachings*
(St. Paul, MN: Llewellyn Publications, 2000), p. 100.

22. From "Summerland" at http://en.wikipedia.org/wiki/The_Summerland.

23. Zimmermann and Gleason, *The Complete Idiot's Guide to Wicca and Witchcraft*, p. 9.

24. Cantrell, *Wiccan Beliefs and Practices*, p. 49.

25. Ibid., p. 59.

26. Ibid., p. 61.

27. Ibid., p. 61.

28. Ibid., pp. 63-70.

29. From "Wicca" at http://en.wikipedia.org/wiki/Wicca.

30. From "Handfasting" at http://en.wikipedia.org/wiki/Handfasting.

31. Scott Cunningham, *The Truth About Witchcraft Today* (St. Paul, MN:
Llewellyn Publications, 1999), p. 77.

32. Ibid., p. 66.

33. Thanks to Michael Gleghorn for his article "Wicca: A Biblical Critique,"
which included these quotes and the information adapted in this section.
Accessed at the Probe Ministries Web site at http://www.probe.org/content/
view/945/65/.

34. Raven Grimassi, *The Wiccan Mysteries: Ancient Origins and Teachings*
(St. Paul, MN: Llewellyn Publications, 2000), p. 26.

35. Ibid., p. 27.

36. Starhawk (Miriam Simos), *The Spiral Dance: A Rebirth of the Ancient Religion of the Great Goddess* (San Francisco, CA: Harper and Row, 1979), p. 14.

37. Michael Gleghorn, "Wicca: A Biblical Critique." Accessed at http://www.probe.org/content/view/945/65/.

38. C.S. Lewis, *The Chronicles of Narnia*, one-volume movie edition (Grand Rapids, MI: Zondervan, 2005), p. 194.

Chapter 8—Kabbalah: A Mystical Judaism?

1. "Madonna—Kabbalah No Fad," November 18, 2004. Accessed at http://www.femalefirst.co.uk/entertainment/12852004.htm.

2. From "Paris Hilton 'Converts to Kabbalah.'" Accessed at http://www.femalefirst.co.uk/celebrity/6852004.htm.

3. Jennifer Minar, "Celebrities and Kabbalah...What's the Fascination?" *Associated Content*, May 17, 2005. Accessed at http://www.associatedcontent.com/article/3010/celebrities_and_kabbalah_why_the_fascination.html.

4. "What Is Kabbalah?" Accessed at http://www.kabbalah.com/01.php.

5. David A. Cooper, *God Is a Verb* (New York: Riverhead Brooks, 1997), p. 11.

6. Rodger Kamenetz, as cited by Arthur Goldwag, *The Beliefnet Guide to Kabbalah* (New York: Doubleday, 2005), p. 154.

7. "Kabbalah Red String" at http://www.kabbalah.com/kabbalah/13.php.

8. Ershom Scholem, *Major Trends in Jewish Mysticism* (New York: Schocken, 1974), p. 136.

9. See the article "What Is a Biblical View of Kabbalah?" at http://www.probe.org/probe-answers-e-mail/cults-and-world-religions/what-is-a-biblical-view-of-kabbalah.html.

10. Deborah Kerdeman and Lawrence Kushner, *The Invisible Chariot* (Denver: A.R.E. Publishing, 1986), p. 90.

11. See the extensive list at "Kabbalah" at http://en.wikipedia.org/wiki/Kabbalah.

12. Accessed at http://www.equip.org/free/dc040.htm.

13. Ibid.

14. Arthur Goldwag, *The Beliefnet Guide to Kabbalah* (New York: Doubleday, 2005), p. 4.

15. From "Kabbalah" at http://en.wikipedia.org/wiki/Kabbalah.

16. Goldwag, *The Beliefnet Guide to Kabbalah*, p. 4.

Part Four: Eastern Religions

1. From http://www.hinduwisdom.info/quotes1_20.htm.

Chapter 9—Hinduism: Everything Is One?

1. From http://www.religioustolerance.org/hinduism.htm.

2. From http://www.adherents.com/Religions_By_Adherents.html. World Hinduism adherent figures are usually between 850 million and one billion.

3. See specific episode information at "Karma" at http://en.wikipedia.org/wiki/Karma#Western_interpretation.

4. The earliest evidence for elements of the Hindu faith is sometimes claimed to date back as far as the late Neolithic to the Early Harappan period (circa 5500–3300 B.C.E.). See BBC's "Religion and Ethics: Hinduism" at http://www.bbc.co.uk/religion/religions/hinduism/history/history_1.shtml.

5. John Ankerberg and John Weldon, *Encyclopedia of New Age Beliefs* (Eugene, OR: Harvest House Publishers, 1996), pp. 216-17.

6. A special thanks to Contender Ministries for their information, which is adapted in this section. See their full treatment at http://contenderministries.org/hinduism/hinduism.php.

7. The following comparisons are adapted from http://www.4truth.net/site/apps/nl/content3.asp?c=hiKXLbPNLrF&b=784491&ct=932107, and *Comparing Christianity with World Religions* by Stephen Cory and Dillon Burroughs (Chicago, IL: Moody Publishing, 2007).

8. Swami Nikilananda, *Vivekananda, the Yogas and Other Words* (New York: Ramakrisna-Vivekananda Center, 1953), p. 885.

9. Ibid., pp. 332, 517.

10. Bruce Bickel and Stan Jantz, *World Religions & Cults 101* (Eugene, OR: Harvest House Publishers, 2002), pp. 156-57.

11. "Yoga Continues Its Popularity, Especially with the Young," *Yoga Magazine,* February 5, 2005. Accessed at http://fitnessbusinesspro.com/news/yoga_popularity_020805/.

12. See http://www.christianyoga.us.

13. See the full article by Michael Gleghorn, "Yoga and Christianity: Are They Compatible?" at http://www.probe.org/content/view/967/65/.

14. Gopi Krishna, "The True Aim of Yoga," *Psychic* magazine, January/February 1973, p. 15. See John Ankerberg and John Weldon, *The Facts on Hinduism* (Eugene, OR: Harvest House Publishers, 1991), pp. 14-17 for additional information regarding yoga's physical and spiritual problems.

Chapter 10—Buddhism: What's with the Enlightenment Thing?

1. World estimates for Buddhism vary between 230 and 500 million, with most around 350 million, according to http://www.adherents.com/Religions_By_Adherents.html.

2. Bruce Bickel and Stan Jantz, *World Religions & Cults 101* (Eugene, OR: Harvest House Publishers, 2002), p. 173.

3. From http://www.pluralism.org/resources/statistics/tradition.php#Buddhism.

4. Patrick Zukeran, "Buddhism." Accessed at http://www.probe.org/content/view/64/65/.

5. Ibid., emphasis added.

6. From "The Noble Eightfold Path" at http://www.thebigview.com/buddhism/eightfoldpath.html (emphasis added).

7. Swearer, *Buddhism*, p. 44.

8. Special thanks to www.thebigview.com for their assistance in explaining these eight concepts.

9. From http://buddhism.about.com/library/blbudfoundations.htm.

10. Swearer, *Buddhism*, p. 44.

11. Davis Taylor and Clark Offner, *The World's Religions*, Norman Anderson, ed. (Downers Grove, IL: InterVarsity, 1975), p. 177.

12. Available online at http://www.accesstoinsight.org/ptf/dhamma/sacca/sacca3/nibbana.html.

13. D.T. Suzuki, *Introduction to Zen Buddhism* (London: Rider & Company, 1949), chapter 2. Accessed online at http://www.geocities.com/upakaascetic/zen_intro.html.

14. Matthew 20:28.

15. Patrick Zukeran, "Buddhism." Accessed at http://www.probe.org/content/view/64/65/.

16. Josh McDowell and Don Stewart, *Handbook of Today's Religions*, accessed online at http://www.greatcom.org/resources/handbook_of_todays_religions/03chap03/default.htm.

Chapter 11—Confucianism, Taoism, and Shintoism: What's with All the -isms?

1. Adapted from statistics at www.adherents.com.

2. Marcus Bach, *Major Religions of the World* (Nashville, TN: Abingdon, 1970), p. 81.

3. These Five Classics can be accessed online at http://www.sacred-texts.com/cfu/index.htm.

4. Access this book online at http://www.wright-house.com/religions/confucius/Analects.html.

5. This book accessed online at http://www.sacred-texts.com/cfu/conf3.htm.

6. Josh McDowell and Don Stewart, *Handbook of Today's Religions*, accessed online at http://www.greatcom.org/resources/handbook_of_todays_religions/03chap04/default.htm.

7. Sir Norman Anderson, *Christianity and World Religions* (Downers Grove, IL: InterVarsity Press, 1984), p. 64.

8. Adapted from "Taoism" in Josh McDowell and Don Stewart, *Handbook of Today's Religions*, accessed online at http://www.greatcom.org/resources/handbook_of_todays_religions/03chap04/default.htm.

9. Judith Horstman, "Tai Chi," accessed at https://www.arthritis.org/resources/ arthritistoday/2000_archives/2000_07_08_taichi.asp.

10. Edwina Gately, as cited in John B. Shea, "The Church and the New Age Movement," August 4, 2005. Accessed at http://www.lifeissues.net/writers/ she/she_16church_newage.html.

11. Wing-Tsit Chan, ed., *A Sourcebook in Chinese Philosophy* (Princeton, NJ: Princeton University Press, 1963), p. 190; as cited in Josh McDowell and Don Stewart, *Handbook of Today's Religions,* accessed online at http://www .greatcom.org/resources/handbook_of_todays_religions/03chap04/default .htm.

12. Maurice Rawlings, *Life-Wish: Reincarnation: Reality or Hoax* (Nashville, TN: Thomas Nelson, 1981).

13. Bruce Bickel and Stan Jantz, *World Religions & Cults 101* (Eugene, OR: Harvest House Publishers, 2002), p. 201.

14. Mark Water, *AMG's Encyclopedia of World Religions, Cults, and the Occult* (Chattanooga, TN: AMG Publishers, 2006), p. 451.

15. "Shinto" at http://en.wikipedia.org/wiki/Shinto#Cultural_effects.

Part Five: Multigod and Anti-God Religions

1. From "Major Religions of the World Ranked by Number of Adherents," accessed at http://www.adherents.com/Religions_By_Adherents.html.

Chapter 12—New Age Religions: What's So New About New Age?

1. George Barna, *The Index of Leading Spiritual Indicators* (Dallas TX: Word, 1996). Quoted at http://www.religioustolerance.org/newage.htm.

2. Bruce Bickel and Stan Jantz, *World Religions & Cults 101* (Eugene, OR: Harvest House Publishers, 2002), p. 216.

3. Russell Chandler, *Understanding the New Age* (Grand Rapids, MI: Zondervan, 1993), pp. 20, 130-33.

4. Carl Raschke, as cited in Mark Water, *AMG's Encyclopedia of World Religions, Cults, and the Occult* (Chattanooga, TN: AMG Publishers, 2006), p. 597.

5. Shirley MacLaine, *Out on a Limb* (Toronto, Canada: Bantam Books, 1983), p.268.

6. John Ankerberg and John Weldon, *Facts on the New Age Movement* (Eugene, OR: Harvest House Publishers, 1988), pp.8-9.

7. B.A. Robinson, "New Age Spirituality," Ontario Consultants on Religious Tolerance, October 2006. Available online at http://www.religioustolerance .org/newage.htm.

8. See "Is *The Secret* Compatible with Biblical Christianity?" from the Ankerberg Theological Research Institute. Accessed at http://www.johnankerberg .org/Articles/media-wise/MW0307W2.htm.

9. Cited in Dave Hunt, "Imagination and Visualization," Ankerberg Theological Research Institute, 2001. Accessed at http://www.johnankerberg.org/Articles/_PDFArchives/new-age/NA2W1201.pdf.

10. Adapted from "The New Age Movement," at http://www.dashhouse.com/sermons/1996/PM/961117.htm.

11. See "Channeling," by John Weldon at http://www.johnankerberg.com/Articles/_PDFArchives/new-age/NA4W1099.pdf.

12. See "Crystal Work," by John Weldon at http://www.johnankerberg.com/Articles/_PDFArchives/new-age/NA3W1199.pdf.

13. See "Divination Practices and Occult Games," by John Ankerberg and John Weldon at http://www.johnankerberg.com/Articles/_PDFArchives/new-age/NA3W1299.pdf.

14. For a comprehensive study on astrology, see John Ankerberg and John Weldon, *Encyclopedia of New Age Beliefs* (Eugene, OR: Harvest House Publishers, 1996), pp. 58-78. Two entire series on astrology are also available at www.johnankerberg.org, entitled "Astrology: Do the Heavens Determine Your Destiny?" and "Astrology: True or False?"

15. See "New Age Medicine, the Nature of the Cures," by John Ankerberg and John Weldon at http://www.johnankerberg.com/Articles/_PDFArchives/new-age/NA1W0600.pdf.

Chapter 13—Agnosticism and Atheism: How Can Someone Have a Religion Without God?

1. Richard Dawkins, *The God Delusion* (New York: Houghton Mifflin, 2006), accessed at http://www.richarddawkins.net/mainPage.php?bodyPage=godDelusion.php.

2. Sam Harris, *Letter to a Christian Nation* (New York: Knopf, 2006), p. 1.

3. Sam Schulman, "Without God, Gall Is Permitted," *The Wall Street Journal*, January 5, 2007, p. W11. Available online at http://www.samharris.org/site/full_text/without-god-gall-is-permitted/.

4. "The New Intolerance," *Christianity Today*, January 25, 2007. Accessed at http://www.christianitytoday.com/ct/2007/february/17.24.html.

5. Jim Holt, "Beyond Belief," *The New York Times*, October 22, 2006. Accessed at http://www.nytimes.com/2006/10/22/books/review/Holt.t.html?ex=1319169600&en=d9a0ba69b41f32df&ei=5088.

6. Mark Water, *AMG's Encyclopedia of World Religions, Cults, and the Occult* (Chattanooga, TN: AMG Publishers, 2006), p. 477.

7. Cited in Mark Water, *AMG's Encyclopedia of World Religions, Cults, and the Occult* (Chattanooga, TN: AMG Publishers, 2006), p. 483.

8. Water, *AMG's Encyclopedia of World Religions, Cults, and the Occult*, p. 477.

9. From http://www.religioustolerance.org/agnostic.htm.

10. Adapted from Austin Cline, "Atheism vs. Agnosticism: What's the Difference? Are they Alternatives to Each Other?" Accessed at http://atheism.about.com/od/aboutagnosticism/a/atheism.htm.

11. Adapted from "Agnosticism" at http://www.religioustolerance.org/agnostic.htm.

12. Thomas H. Huxley, *Christianity and Agnosticism: A Controversy* (New York: D. Appleton and Company, 1889). Accessed online at http://www.infidels.org/library/historical/.

13. R.G. Ingersoll, *Why I Am an Agnostic,* cited at http://www.religioustolerance.org/agnostic.htm.

14. Bertrand Russell, *The Autobiography of Bertrand Russell* (London: Routledge, 1998), p. 257.

15. Water, *AMG's Encyclopedia of World Religions, Cults, and the Occult,* p. 481.

16. Norman Geisler, *Christian Apologetics* (Grand Rapids, MI: Baker Book House, 1976), p. 20.

17. Austin Cline, "Agnosticism vs. Atheism," at http://atheism.about.com/od/aboutagnosticism/a/atheism.htm.

18. Cited in Ravi Zacharias, *The Real Face of Atheism* (Grand Rapids, MI: Baker Books, 2004), p. 19.

19. From http://blog.christianitytoday.com/outofur/archives/2006/04/the_ebay_atheis.html.

20. Adapted from Norman Geisler, *Baker Encyclopedia of Christian Apologetics* (Grand Rapids, MI: Zondervan, 1999), pp. 55-56.

21. Norman Geisler, *Baker Encyclopedia of Christian Apologetics* (Grand Rapids, MI: Zondervan, 1999), p. 283.

Conclusion: Where Do We Grow from Here?

1. Isaiah 53:6 NLT.

2. Isaiah 59:2 NLT.

3. Ezekiel 18:4.

4. Matthew 25:31-46; John 5:21-29.

5. Isaiah 53:6 NLT.

6. Isaiah 53:5 NLT.

7. Isaiah 53:12 NLT.

8. 1 Peter 3:18 NLT.

9. Isaiah 55:6-7 NLT.

10. John 5:24 NLT.

11. John 17:3 NLT.

12. Ephesians 2:8-9 NLT.

Appendix—Biblical Warnings Against Occult Involvement

1. Reprinted by permission from the Ankerberg Theological Research Institute, © 2005. Accessed online at http://www.johnankerberg.org/Articles/_PDFArchives/media-wise/MW3W0405A.pdf.

2. Alexander Brooks, "What Is Spiritualism…and Why Are They Saying Those Awful Things About It?" (Berkeley, CA: Spiritual Counterfeits Project, 1986), p. 3.

About the Authors

John Ankerberg, host of the award-winning *John Ankerberg Show,* has three earned degrees: a Master of Arts in church history and the philosophy of Christian thought, a Master of Divinity from Trinity International University, and a Doctor of Ministry from Luther Rice Seminary. With Dr. John Weldon, he has coauthored *What Do Mormons Really Believe?, Fast Facts on Islam,* the "Facts on" Series of apologetic booklets, and other resources.

Dillon Burroughs, a full-time writer who has worked with a number of bestselling authors, is a graduate of Dallas Theological Seminary and coauthor of *Middle East Meltdown* (middleeastmeltdown.com) with John Ankerberg. Dillon is a graduate of Dallas Theological Seminary and lives in Tennessee with his wife, Deborah, and their two children.

HARVEST HOUSE
PUBLISHERS

Harvest House Books by
John Ankerberg and Dillon Burroughs

Middle East Meltdown

What's the Big Deal About Jesus?

What Can Be Found in Lost?

What's the Big Deal About Other Religions?

Harvest House Books by
John Ankerberg and John Weldon

Creation vs. Evolution: What You Need to Know

Fast Facts® on Defending Your Faith

Fast Facts® on Islam

Fast Facts® on Jehovah's Witnesses

Fast Facts® on Momonism

Fast Facts® on the Masonic Lodge

The Facts on Halloween

The Facts on Homosexuality

The Facts on Islam

The Facts on Jehovah's Witnesses

The Facts on Roman Catholicism

The Facts on the King James Only Debate

The Facts on the Masonic Lodge

The Facts on the Mormon Church

The Facts on Why You Can Believe the Bible

The Facts on World Religions

CPSIA information can be obtained
at www.ICGtesting.com
Printed in the USA
BVHW061149261222
654949BV00036B/1680

9 780736 921220